# OAK HILL COUNTRY CLUB

## *A Legacy of Golfing Excellence*

SAL MAIORANA

THE History PRESS

Published by The History Press
Charleston, SC 29403
www.historypress.net



All photos courtesy of the Oak Hill Historian's Office unless otherwise noted.

First published 2013

Manufactured in the United States

ISBN 978.1.62619.037.5

Library of Congress CIP data applied for.

*Notice*: The information in this book is true and complete to the best of our knowledge. It is offered without guarantee on the part of the author or The History Press. The author and The History Press disclaim all liability in connection with the use of this book.

# Contents

# Acknowledgements

I owe a tremendous debt of gratitude to the Oak Hill membership and board of directors, which has always cooperated and supported projects such as this.

This is a club with a wildly fascinating history—one that it has always embraced and reveled in. By offering use of its vast collection of photographs (which is second to none) and with the help of longtime members spending time sharing their recollections, Oak Hill has allowed me to tell its story in as comprehensive a manner as possible.

A very special thanks to Mary Szpak, who runs the operation in the historian's office. No matter what I needed, Mary was right there to track it down using the club's extensive computer database of photos and artifacts. She is an invaluable resource to the club.

To members and personal friends Bill Reeves, Jerry Stahl, Bill Westerfeld, Bill Thaney Sr. and the late Allen Brewer, your knowledge and perspective regarding the club and its history of hosting major tournaments lent monumental assistance to my research.

Many thanks to head pro Craig Harmon, greens superintendent Jeff Corcoran, past greens super Joe Hahn, Jeff Sluman, Terry Diehl, Jack Nicklaus, Lee Trevino, Eric Rule, Dan Farrell, Bob Hoff, Don Kladstrup, Fred Beltz and the late Sam Urzetta for answering my interview requests and delivering such thoughtful insight.

And thanks to the folks at The History Press, especially commissioning editor Whitney Tarella Landis for contacting me and recruiting me to author this history, project editor Will Collicott for his thorough work on the manuscript and sales representative Dani McGrath.

*Chapter 1*

# A Paradise in Pittsford

The late Martin Gullen, a former president of Oak Hill Country Club and one of its most influential members, once expressed in a letter to the membership his feelings about the plot of paradise in Pittsford that, by the late 1960s, had become known as one of the jewels of Rochester. It read in part:

> *To enter between the rows of firs and oaks, to view the majestic clubhouse in English Tudor style, to dine with impeccable service and then go out into the sunshine and see the magnificent golf courses with lush trees and fairways and velvety greens is an experience never to be forgotten. It becomes a treasured memory to be repeated as often as a man possibly can.*

That eloquent synopsis was penned more than forty years ago, and Oak Hill has only grown more majestic and magnificent in the intervening decades, its status as one of the finest golf clubs in America (and yes, the world) undeniably secure. "Oak Hill has always been a great golf course, one I've always enjoyed playing," said Jack Nicklaus, the man some still consider the greatest golfer of them all. "I think it's one of the good, old, solid golf courses in this country."

But it wasn't always this way.

In the fall of 1901, a group of twenty-five men came together to discuss establishing a new golf club for the city of Rochester. Their commonality was quite obvious: all were affluent and prominent community leaders with well-minded civic goals and pride. Among them were Jeremiah Hickey, the co-founder of Hickey-Freeman Co.; George W. Aldridge, a Republican Party political heavyweight; Dr. George W. Goler, one of the country's leading public health officers; Judge Arthur E. Sutherland; and Irving Robeson, who ran the Rochester Stamping Company and was one of the finest golfers in the region.

Their meeting led to the incorporation of the club on October 2, 1901, and they agreed to lease—with the intention of ultimately purchasing—an eighty-five-acre parcel of land, not in Pittsford but next to the Genesee River, where the University of Rochester is now located. It was the most humble of beginnings, unpretentious in every way—a hardscrabble nine-hole layout on mostly barren farmland (save for the occasional oak tree) with a converted farmhouse that did not have hot water and was illuminated by kerosene lamps serving as the clubhouse.

The original Oak Hill endured many financial hardships in its first twenty years, and assessments were routinely meted out in an effort to erase the seemingly perpetual red ink on the books. Yet Oak Hill persevered because the members could see that the capital improvements were transforming their club into one of the centerpieces of Rochester, thus allowing it to mirror the prosperity of the city.

Then, just as Oak Hill was establishing firm roots in the downtown location, an intriguing proposal was put forth, and a historic real estate deal was transacted that ultimately proved enormously beneficial—not only to Oak Hill but also to the University of Rochester and, by extension, the city itself. The university, originally located on Prince Street, was growing in stature worldwide and needed an expansion after George Eastman, the founder of the Eastman Kodak Company, made clear his intention of using a portion of his voluminous wealth to fund the building of a music school and a medical center.

Many locations were scouted, but it was decided that the ideal spot for the new campus was on the land along the river occupied by Oak Hill. After tedious discussions, Oak Hill agreed to pull up its stakes, as its members, blessed with foresight and business acumen, recognized a great opportunity. For relinquishing its property, Oak Hill was bequeathed 355 acres of farmland in the town of Pittsford, and the university agreed to pay for the design and construction of two eighteen-hole courses and a spectacular Tudor-style clubhouse, an outlay of about $360,000. Speaking for a membership that clearly understood the benefits of this deal, both for Oak Hill and the university, then–Oak Hill president Clarence Wheeler

The original Oak Hill site was located in downtown Rochester, and one of its borders was the Genesee River.

said, "We cannot do otherwise than give way to such a tremendous project for the good of the city."

Famed golf course architect Donald Ross was hired to design the two golf courses, while Oak Hill member Dr. John R. Williams quit his medical practice to devote the rest of his life to beautifying the grounds of the new Oak Hill by planting between thirty thousand and forty thousand trees. And then Mother Nature took over and created a masterpiece. From those little acorns that Dr. Williams planted, Oak Hill blossomed breathtakingly. And once the East Course began playing host to major tournaments such as the U.S. Amateur and the U.S. Open, that splendor was on display for all to see, just as it will be in August 2013, when the PGA Championship will be contested there for the third time.

The greatest names in golf have competed on the East Course—Nicklaus, Ben Hogan, Sam Snead, Byron Nelson, Arnold Palmer, Lee Trevino, Tiger Woods—and the lowest seventy-two-hole score ever posted there was six-under-par by Nicklaus in the 1980 PGA Championship, a testament to the enduring challenge that Oak Hill has always presented. "There is no let-up hole on the golf course, and that's something proud to be said," said Curtis Strange, who won the 1989 U.S. Open at Oak Hill. "Every hole seems to be a good golf hole."

Throughout its century-plus existence, Oak Hill has been a dream come true for the Rochester and Monroe County Chambers of Commerce. It is a beacon of brilliant beauty that has attracted the attention of the world and shone a glaring spotlight on the region.

For those fortunate enough to be or have been members of Oak Hill, and for those who have had the privilege of being guests even for just a day, it is an experience that, as Gullen said, should be enjoyed as often as possible. "It is a way of life for those who savor fine sport like a vintage wine, presented in a setting of matchless beauty, calculated to obscure the stress and turmoil of the modern world," Gullen wrote in that long-ago letter. "An afternoon at Oak Hill, where so many splendors greet the eye, is a visit to the carefree past, the era of the sidewalk café, the park carriage and the leisurely pace. The men who built Oak Hill had something money can't buy. They had taste."

*Chapter 2*

# Birthplace by the Genesee River

Golf met America as the nineteenth century was transitioning into the twentieth, and Rochester was awash in a period of tremendous growth and prosperity.

The continued westward settlement of the United States led to the discovery of the rich wheat fields in the Great Plains that eventually deprived Rochester of its once-lofty position as the premier flour center in the country. Yet while the number of flour mills had been dwindling since the end of the Civil War, other businesses were thriving during a time when governmental interference and heavy taxation were not a detriment to operations.

By 1890, there were nine railroads passing through Rochester. Annual imports and exports through the lake port of Charlotte both topped out at about $1 million, and more than 400,000 tons of merchandise were being loaded and unloaded yearly from the canal. Horticulture was also at its peak, as nurseries along East Avenue were in perpetual bloom, filling orders domestically as well as internationally. Once known as the "Flour City," Rochester was now being referred to as the "Flower City."

It was also during this time that John Jacob Bausch and Henry Lomb perfected the production of optical lenses. There were approximately thirty clothing factories and about sixty shoe factories employing thousands of people, while other citizens worked as foundry men, tobacco processors, bankers and accountants. But the Eastman Kodak Company, founded in 1889 by George Eastman following his invention of the Kodak camera,

The members approved the building of a magnificent and expansive new clubhouse. It was completed in 1911.

had begun to set industry standards in photography and would ultimately become Rochester's largest employer.

Like most cities of that era, Rochester was hard at work and found little time to play. Culturally, citizens flocked to the Powers Gallery, which was considered the center of the city's artistic life, and there were numerous

The first clubhouse, circa 1905, was a converted farmhouse that was already on the grounds when the property was purchased.

music, theater and literary clubs. Outdoor recreation and athletic activity consisted mainly of hunting and fishing, rowing along the river, ice skating at the Aqueduct and baseball.

But there was also this new game—this odd pursuit in which men would swing a wooden-shafted stick with a metal flange attached to the end and strike a gutta-percha ball sitting on the ground, propelling it as much as one hundred or more yards at a time. Then they would go find the ball, striking it again and again before eventually sweeping it subtly into a hole a mere four inches in circumference—the fewer strokes the better.

Europeans had been playing golf for hundreds of years, but the sport had only arrived on this side of the Atlantic in the late 1880s in a few select spots, and one of those was Rochester—thanks in large part, as legend has it, to a tobacco magnate named William S. Kimball.

Kimball was among Rochester's foremost businessmen, one of the largest employers of women in the city and also the man who commissioned the statue of Mercury that was originally perched on the roof of his tobacco factory and now resides atop the Thomson West building downtown on Broad Street. In the summer of 1892, Kimball read about this game called golf and, eager to learn more, convinced four of his friends who were vacationing in Nantucket to meet him in New York City, where golf had already taken hold, so they could try their hand at it.

Kimball and his friends were enthralled, and the following spring, they took it upon themselves to lay out Rochester's first golf course in Genesee

Valley Park using flower pots as cups. Appropriately, they are believed to be the first Rochesterians to play on the city's inaugural course. Soon, many of their colleagues and friends caught the bug, and this spike in interest led to them founding the Country Club of Rochester (CCR) in 1895. It was just the fiftieth club in the United States that included a golf course.

Having watched for nearly six years the activity at CCR and realizing the exclusivity and amenities that belonging to a club provided, the original twenty-five founding members of Oak Hill brought their club to fruition, thus providing the city another option to scratch its golf itch. They spread the word about Oak Hill by explaining the benefits of joining to their friends, relatives, neighbors and business associates, and by the time the golf course was ready for play in the spring of 1902, the membership had swelled to 137.

The initiation fee to join was set at $25, with an additional $5 levied for each person attached to the membership, and yearly dues were $20. You might say that was a bargain, given that today's initiation fee ranges upward of $60,000. For their money, members were granted golfing privileges, use of the clubhouse for dinners and club functions, easy access to the river for boating and canoeing and the ever-present camaraderie and friendship of their fellow members.

Though the rules of the day forbade smoking in the clubhouse and drinking or gambling anywhere on the property, the members did not seem to care, and Oak Hill quickly became a haven for social activity and recreation. The prohibition of those squalid habits encouraged a more prudent family atmosphere that would become a key ingredient in the flourishing of Oak Hill. Then, as it is now, Oak Hill was more than just a place to play golf.

Finances were difficult in those first years, but in 1905, it was decided that the club should purchase the land, a combination of two farms owned by the estates of the Adlington and Wolcott families. The price was $34,000, a noteworthy amount given that Oak Hill was in debt by approximately $4,500. But the members firmly believed that what they had at Oak Hill was something special and worth the risk of incurring further financial strain.

In addition to buying the land, plans went ahead to add a porch to the clubhouse. To help defray these costs, dues were raised to forty dollars per year, and a non-golfing membership was introduced at a rate of twenty dollars per month on top of a ten-dollar initiation fee, thus allowing families without an interest in golf the opportunity to enjoy Oak Hill's societal pleasures.

Membership was growing steadily and by 1907 had reached about 250. But despite the popularity of the club, monetary difficulties persisted, and two previous club treasurers had quit, reportedly because the pressure of the job was too great as they tried to operate on an annual budget of about $21,000. In 1908, guest fees were reduced to fifty cents per round in the hope that more rounds would be played, thus increasing revenue. But that plan couldn't raise enough money even for the club to splurge on hiring professional musicians to provide entertainment at certain functions.

Through it all, one thing remained undeterred at Oak Hill: its spirit. The members reveled in the ever-growing regional significance of Oak Hill, and they were prepared to do whatever it took to ensure the viability of what they had created. This was evident in 1910 when the members approved two seismic projects that indicated there was no turning back now: the construction of a second nine holes to bring the golf course up to the traditional eighteen-hole standard, and a sparkling new clubhouse that would cost more than $70,000. Dues and initiation fees were raised to $50, and the dues quickly climbed to $75, with each member also asked to pay a $50 assessment in order to help foot the bill. The new structure opened on Memorial Day 1911 and included a wraparound porch, a social hall, a dining room that seated 450 and eighteen bedrooms for overnight guests.

For much of the next decade, Oak Hill surged ahead, even as the country plunged wholly into the Great War. Golf was gaining rapid popularity in Rochester and across the country, in no small part because of the exploits of a flamboyant soul from East Rochester named Walter Hagen, who had gained international fame for winning the U.S. Open in 1914 and then again in 1919. Oak Hill's roll call counted some of the most powerful men in the city, and they were enjoying a course that had begun to develop character and challenging maturity through careful landscaping and nurturing.

So it was no surprise that as the magnificent decade of the 1920s came roaring in, Oak Hill's membership was highly skeptical of the controversial real estate proposal that would wipe out more than twenty years of equity and force the club to start from scratch in a new location—one that at the time wasn't nearly as desirable as the perch hard by the Genesee.

*Chapter 3*

# A HISTORIC REAL ESTATE DEAL

When George Eastman, the father of modern photography and one of the nation's foremost philanthropists, could no longer endure the nonstop pain associated with a degenerative spinal condition and committed suicide on March 14, 1932, he left a simple note that read, "To my friends: my work is done, why wait?"

It was a sad ending to the life of Rochester's patriarch and one of America's most influential citizens. But before that self-inflicted gunshot pierced his heart, Eastman created a colossal legacy that has continued to thrive more than eight decades since he was laid to rest in Kodak Park on the grounds where his Eastman Kodak Company originated.

Although Eastman Kodak, once the world leader in all things photographic as well as Rochester's largest employer, has stumbled into bankruptcy and is barely a shell of itself, twenty-first-century Rochester still benefits from the incalculable generosity of Eastman in the form of the University of Rochester campus, Strong Memorial Hospital, the Eastman School of Music, the Eastman Theater, the George Eastman House and several landmark buildings that were made possible through his benevolence.

And of course, there is Oak Hill.

"George Eastman had as his primary objective putting a university along the Genesee River, and everything he did had a very definite purpose," said Tom Mooney, an Oak Hill member and the former president of the Rochester Chamber of Commerce. "That was an example of Eastman moving to achieve what he thought was going to be something very

George Eastman, who founded the Eastman Kodak Company, was one of Rochester's most distinguished citizens, and his philanthropy played a key role in Oak Hill moving to its Pittsford home.

good for the community, but he actually produced a double benefit. He was able to move the university to the river, but I don't think he anticipated that in the swap of the land, he was creating another jewel for the community and, really, a jewel for the world of golf right here in the Rochester region."

In actuality, Eastman had virtually nothing to do with the creation of the new Oak Hill in Pittsford. But it was his involvement with the reinvention of the new University of Rochester (UR) that led to the transplantation of Oak Hill to the suburbs, where it ultimately flourished into one of the world's most beautiful golf courses. The story has become part of Rochester's rich lore, and it starts nearly two decades before the historic land swap was consummated in 1924.

Rush Rhees, a forty-four-year-old Baptist preacher and professor of the New Testament, became the university's president in 1900. This man, blessed with broad vision, could recognize even then that the current site downtown on Prince Street was too antiquated for the growth the school was enjoying and the big plans he was hoping to implement.

Rhees first approached Eastman in 1903 to seek funding for a biology and physics building. The projected cost, including equipping the facility, was about $150,000, and Rhees was hoping that Eastman would pledge the entire sum. Instead, Eastman offered $10,000. As Rhees was leaving Eastman's mansion on East Avenue, Eastman said, "You're disappointed, aren't you?" Rhees admitted that he was, but he graciously shook hands and did not pester Eastman any further. That was the best thing Rhees could have done because that impressed Eastman and prompted him to write a check for $60,000. In the end, the total cost of the project wound up being about $78,000, and Eastman did indeed foot the entire bill. It was the

University of Rochester president Rush Rhees breaks ground as construction of the university begins.

beginning of a relationship that UR still benefits from more than a century later.

Earlier in his life, when he was just beginning to accumulate his massive wealth, Eastman had stated that he was not in favor of higher education. He was a self-made man who believed that hard work and training through trial and error was how men became successful. So this gift to Rhees was considered a momentous breakthrough, and as the years progressed and their friendship grew stronger, Eastman changed his philosophy and ultimately provided gifts totaling more than $51 million to the university.

It was in early 1920 when Rhees informed his good friend, architect George W. Todd, that Eastman was interested in funding the building of the medical school and music school for the university. Coincidentally, Todd had been working through a brainstorm regarding the building of a new campus, and his sights were set on the Oak Hill property along the river. Todd and Rhees laid out their idea to Eastman, and after expressing strong opposition because he favored expanding the Prince Street location, Eastman was converted.

When the influential threesome went public with the idea, there was tremendous debate on the topic. For instance, UR trustee Harper Sibley preferred a location on Lake Ontario in the town of Webster, while his father, Hiram, wanted to make the university "the crowning glory of East Avenue." There was also talk of a five-hundred-acre plot along Irondequoit Bay and another site in the city near Highland Park where the Colgate-Rochester Divinity School was later built.

After much handwringing, Rhees wielded the ultimate power and declared it was going to be "Oak Hill or nothing." After more than a year of ironing out the particulars and Todd organizing a committee charged with procuring $10 million in donations, it was time to negotiate with Oak Hill for the relinquishment of the property. The talks were tedious and protracted, but the deal was ultimately struck, and final ratification of the historic agreement came on April 4, 1924.

The members of Oak Hill loved their club and its location, and many had built more than twenty years of memories along the riverside. But these men did not achieve their lofty financial, business and community status without being blessed with intelligence, foresight and civic awareness. They recognized a golden opportunity that would ultimately benefit Oak Hill, the university and the city. By allowing the small arts and sciences college a chance to grow into a prestigious institution, the quality of life in Rochester would only improve. As for Oak Hill, this was a chance to start anew—a chance to build the club exactly the way the members wanted.

At the time, the land swap was called "Rochester's greatest achievement." Given that the university has become one of the finest in the nation and that Oak Hill, by the end of 2013, will have played host to three U.S. Opens, three PGA Championships, two U.S. Amateurs, one Ryder Cup, one U.S. Senior Open and one Senior PGA, that could now be viewed as an understatement of titanic proportion.

*Opposite, top*: View of the back of the spectacular Tudor-style clubhouse in the early 1930s.

*Opposite, bottom*: Oak Hill president Clarence Wheeler inserts the first shovel at the Pittsford groundbreaking.

*Chapter 4*

# Right Man for the Job

Almost immediately after Rhees, Todd and Eastman presented their proposal to Oak Hill, club officials—even before they had decided whether to agree to the terms—began contacting prospective golf course architects to gauge whether the Pittsford property was suitable. One of the men brought in to share an opinion was Donald Ross, a Scotsman who had already become one of the world's foremost in the field. After surveying the site in May 1922, Ross reported to the membership that there were great possibilities and that he believed the mostly barren and beaten farmland could be made into "one of the finest golf courses in the United States," mainly because of the rolling terrain and the way Allen's Creek meandered through the landscape.

After reviewing routing sketches that Ross inked on napkins from the Seneca Hotel (where he lodged during his stay) that included two separate courses named the East Eighteen and the West Eighteen, Oak Hill moved quickly and retained his services in anticipation of what was now an inevitable outcome: the transfer from the riverside downtown to the untapped expanse of Pittsford.

Born in Dornoch, Scotland, in 1872, Ross completed his primary schooling and then served a five-year apprenticeship as a carpenter. During this time, Ross did odd jobs at the Dornoch Golf Club and developed a passion for the game. When he was fourteen years old, his first golf mentor, Dornoch Club secretary John Sutherland, brought in four-time British Open champion "Old Tom" Morris to design a second nine holes, and it is believed that Ross met Morris at that time and was inspired by his work.

Donald Ross was considered the preeminent golf course architect during the first half of the twentieth century.

In the early 1890s, Ross decided that he wanted to pursue a career in golf, and Sutherland set him on the proper course. He wrote to the club secretaries at St. Andrews and Carnoustie, imploring them to allow Ross to train under their professionals in the art of clubmaking and greenskeeping, which were the primary responsibilities of club pros. Ross was mentored by a number of men, including Morris at St. Andrews, and in the mid-1890s, at the request of Sutherland, Dornoch hired Ross to become its first professional.

As longtime Oak Hill member and Hill of Fame chairman Bill Reeves wrote in his dedication remarks when Ross was inducted into the Hill of Fame in 1994:

> *The influences of Sutherland and Morris, and the influence of his upbringing in the community of Dornoch, had produced not only a skilled professional but also a man of immense character and integrity. By the end of this period, Donald Ross had been formed and shaped in the same way that, as a clubmaker, he had formed and shaped raw wood into beautiful wooden clubs, and in the same way that later, as a golf course architect, he would form and shape raw land into golf courses of magnificent and timeless design.*

In 1898, a Harvard professor named Robert Wilson went to Dornoch to play, and he explained to Ross that golf was becoming popular in the United States and that he thought Ross could make sixty dollars a month and fifty cents per lesson. Wilson said he could get Ross a job at the Oakley Golf Club in Massachusetts. Ross leaped at the chance and came to the United States the following year.

While at Oakley, Ross met James Tufts, inventor of the soda fountain, who was planning to build a wintertime golf mecca in Pinehurst, North Carolina. Tufts hired Ross as his manager of golf, and this led to Ross's design of the course he always considered his greatest accomplishment—Pinehurst No. 2. Word of Ross's excellence in course design began to spread, and soon he was being commissioned by clubs all across the country.

A fine player in his own right, Ross found time to win the inaugural North-South Amateur at Pinehurst in 1903 and two Massachusetts state opens. He also competed in seven U.S. Opens (finishing in the top ten four times between 1902 and 1907) and returned to Scotland to play in the 1910 British Open at St. Andrews, in which he placed tenth.

But by 1916, Ross had decided to devote all of his attention solely to course design and construction, and figures indicate that between 1916 and 1931, he was involved with 342 courses, including nationally known Oak Hill, Oakland Hills, Pinehurst, Inverness, Seminole, Scioto and Interlachen, as well as Rochester's Monroe, Brook-Lea, Irondequoit (nine holes in 1916) and CCR (redesign work). In all, it is believed that Ross designed 413 courses in America, and the only states in the union in which Ross, who died in 1948, claims he did not put his work on display were Arizona, Utah and Montana (obviously Hawaii and Alaska have since been added to that short list). Among his signatures were crowned greens, providing openings to the green, never placing bunkers behind the green and keeping sand off the bunker faces, all of which remain in evidence at Oak Hill. "We had a great designer—Donald Ross," said Oak Hill member Don Kladstrup, the now-retired club historian. "We still prize, of course, that many of our holes are essentially the way he designed them with little change since then. A few have had some changes, but there's a lot of Donald Ross out here, and I'm talking about on both courses—East and West." It is a remarkable testament to Ross's skill that even in an era when many of the old courses have been rendered pitch-and-putts by new-age equipment that has changed the way the game is played, many of his layouts—like both courses at Oak Hill—have stood the test of time, science and the modern-day athlete.

Curtis Strange noted of Oak Hill:

> *The grand old courses can still hold their own. I call Oak Hill one of the original hard golf courses. You play it basically the way the members*

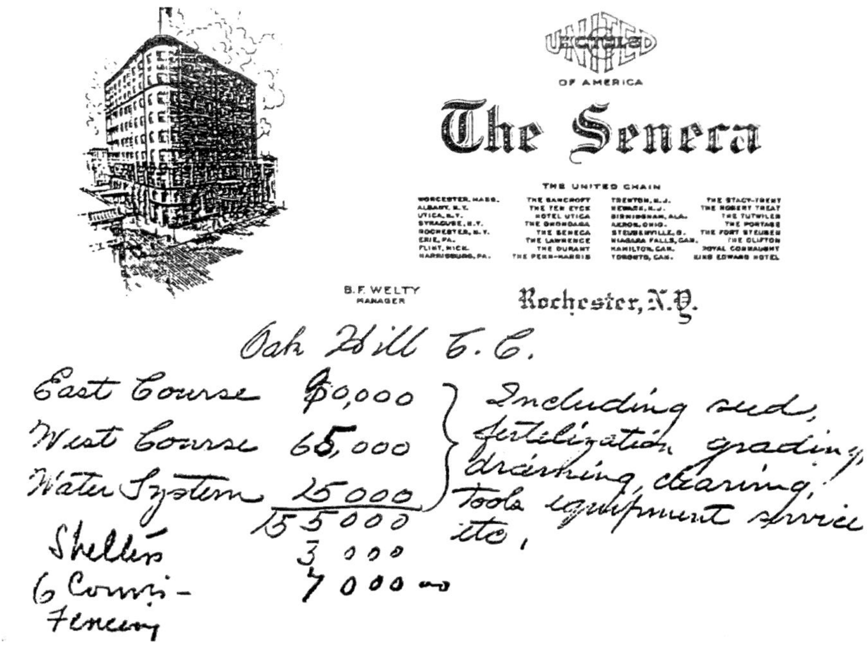

United of America

The Seneca

THE UNITED CHAIN

| | | | |
|---|---|---|---|
| WORCESTER, MASS. | THE BANCROFT | TRENTON, N.J. | THE STACY-TRENT |
| ALBANY, N.Y. | THE TEN EYCK | NEWARK, N.J. | THE ROBERT TREAT |
| UTICA, N.Y. | HOTEL UTICA | BIRMINGHAM, ALA. | THE TUTWILER |
| SYRACUSE, N.Y. | THE ONONDAGA | AKRON, OHIO. | THE PORTAGE |
| ROCHESTER, N.Y. | THE SENECA | STEUBENVILLE, O. | THE FORT STEUBEN |
| ERIE, PA. | THE LAWRENCE | NIAGARA FALLS, CAN. | THE CLIFTON |
| FLINT, MICH. | THE DURANT | HAMILTON, CAN. | ROYAL CONNAUGHT |
| HARRISBURG, PA. | THE PENN-HARRIS | TORONTO, CAN. | KING EDWARD HOTEL |

B.F. WELTY
MANAGER

Rochester, N.Y.

Oak Hill C.C.

East Course $[illegible]0,000
West Course 65,000
Water System 25000
155000
Shelters 3000
6 Comfi- Fencing 7000

Including seed, fertilization, grading, draining, clearing, tools equipment service etc.

While staying at the Seneca Hotel during a visit to Rochester, architect Donald Ross jotted down some notes regarding cost estimates to build Oak Hill's two courses.

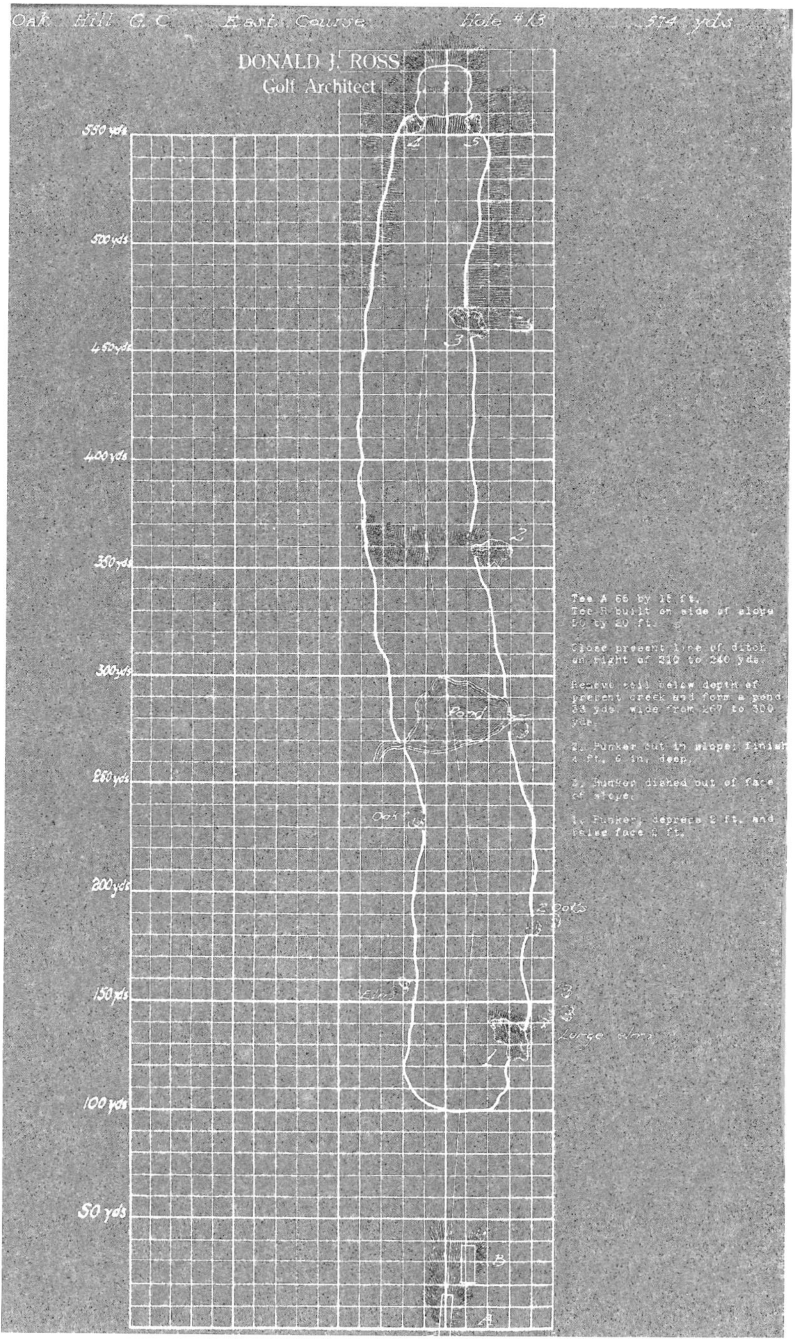


Donald Ross's design drawing for the thirteenth hole on the East Course.

*play it every day. You don't have to do much to it at all for the major championships. You grow the rough, you speed up the greens and it's good to go. There is no let-up hole on the golf course, and that's something proud to be said. Every hole seems to be a good golf hole.*

Ross explained his design standards this way:

*Make each hole present a different problem; arrange the layout so that every stroke must be made with a full concentration and attention necessary to good golf; build each hole in a manner that it wastes none of the ground at my disposal and takes advantage of every possibility I can see. In laying out a course, the cardinal rule is to make the holes so the man who plays it as he should gets par, and the man who makes a mistake makes one more than par. The ideal course is one that presents a test of golf for the everyday golfer and the first-class golfer.*

Ross, who was the first architect inducted into the World Golf Hall of Fame in 1977, once said, "The Lord made golf courses; golf architects simply discover them." But everywhere he went, Ross augmented the Lord's handiwork in brilliant and breathtaking fashion. "I grew up on a Donald Ross golf course," said Jack Nicklaus, referring to Scioto in Columbus, Ohio. "Donald Ross is a great architect. I suppose he's sort of the granddaddy of golf course design."

*Chapter 5*

# Creating Green Mansions

As you scan down the list of world-renowned courses that Ross designed in the United States, it is hard to imagine that the man really didn't have much use for trees. He could do wondrous things with hills and valleys and creeks and ponds, utilizing every inch available on his earthly canvas to craft a unique challenge on every hole. But he would often remove trees during his routing rather than utilize them for scenery or even boundaries. "As beautiful as trees are, and as fond as you and I are of them, we still must not lose sight of the fact that there is limited place for them in golf," Ross once said. "We must not allow our sentiments to crowd out the real intent of a golf course, that of providing fair playing conditions. If it in any way interferes with a properly played stroke, I think the tree is an unfair hazard and should not be allowed to stand." An intriguing statement from a man who was so obviously in touch with nature's beauty, but it's not far fetched when you remember that Ross was raised in northern Scotland, where trees had almost no place (and still don't) on the links courses there.

Still, as marvelous and timeless as Ross's designs of the East and West Courses were, can anyone imagine Oak Hill without the abundance of trees that were planted and nurtured by legendary member Dr. John R. Williams? Of course not. And the guess is that Ross, too, would today be enamored with the trees at Oak Hill because Dr. Williams did such a masterful job of incorporating them into the layouts so as none "interfere with properly played strokes."

As Ross went about sculpting what would become yet another masterpiece on his résumé, the Oak Hill membership continued to play on its original

Dr. John R. Williams (right) chats with legendary American amateur and 1913 U.S. Open champion Francis Ouimet.

course by the river, waiting anxiously to see the final product. Approximately 165 men worked on the project, and using fifty-four teams of horses, six tractors and two steam shovels, they moved about 200,000 cubic yards of earth, installed more than sixteen miles of drainage tile and five miles of cast iron plumbing, built fourteen bridges and planted 26,000 pounds of grass seed. At a final cost of about $167,000, the thirty-six holes were completed in the fall of 1926, and the members pushed their first tees into the freshly groomed land shortly thereafter.

The membership was thrilled with what Ross had created, but it was also apparent that the mostly desolate Pittsford land lacked character, much like the original Oak Hill site. The soil had been beaten badly by more than one hundred years of farming, and the lack of trees prompted one onlooker to

Clarence Wheeler, a multi-term Oak Hill president, fully supported Dr. John R. Williams's tree-planting strategy.

remark that the new Oak Hill was "barren, cheerless and lacking in singular beauty." Dr. Williams felt the same way. So after surveying the new playground, he decided to undertake the Herculean task of enhancing Ross's magnificent layouts (despite his thriving medical practice and his status as one of the nation's leading research physicians) by planting trees. And not just a few, but tens of thousands of oaks, maples, evergreens, spruces, more oaks, Douglas firs, elms, Babylon willows, pines, more oaks and many more species to line and define the neatly contoured fairways. "Every time I walk around Oak Hill and look around, I always think about the man who had the foresight to do this," Dr. Tom Rodenhouse, an Oak Hill member, said of the man whom former *Democrat* and *Chronicle* outdoors writer Floyd King once described as having the "agelessness of the Sequoia and the rugged stamina and integrity of the oak."

Dr. Williams was born in Renfrew, Ontario, in 1874, but his family moved to the United States and settled in Rochester when he was a young boy. He was educated in the city's public school system before attending the University of Michigan, where he earned a doctorate in medicine and graduated first in his 1903 class. He could have gone to so many places, but he returned to Rochester and became one of the city's most estimable citizens.

In between treating patients, Dr. Williams, a founder of Highland Hospital who served there as chief of medicine for many years until his retirement in 1949, undertook a number of projects that benefited Rochester and, ultimately, the world. He was a pioneer in the area of home food storage. He surveyed seven thousand Rochester homes and discovered that none had a suitable method for storing food that would prevent germs from multiplying.

He outlined standards for refrigeration that were used on U.S. Naval ships and eventually led to the invention of the home refrigerator, as Dr. Williams was dubbed "the father of home refrigeration." He also studied the system by which milk was delivered to homes. In 1912, he borrowed an electric

Aerial view in the early 1940s overlooking the East Course. Just above the pool is the thirteenth green, before the Hill of Fame was surrounded by trees.

truck and sent volunteers from the University of Rochester into the Baden Street section of the city. What they discovered was that milk dealers were covering too wide a territory, thus charging high delivery fees for an often substandard product. National reform of dairies and delivery systems followed quickly.

In 1916, Williams helped establish the country's first laboratory devoted to the study of diabetes. An associate from Toronto, F.C. Banning, discovered insulin, and in 1923, Dr. Williams became the first U.S. doctor to administer the drug to diabetics.

While his achievements were vast and noteworthy, transforming Oak Hill into the arboreal landmark it has become is what most members past and present associate him with. "He devoted the latter part of his life to the landscaping and the beautification of Oak Hill," said Bill Reeves. "He became a world-renowned arborist and horticulturist, and he brought trees—rare varieties of trees—here from all over the world and supervised their planting. It was very interesting because I don't think Dr. Williams ever played golf, but his sole interest was the landscaping of Oak Hill and turning it from the wasteland that it was when we first came here into the place of beauty that it is today."

Dr. Williams consulted with experts in the field, studied climatic conditions, read books and spoke with historians. Working with a bare-bones budget that included his personal money as well as donations from fellow members who supported his efforts (much of that procured by multiple-term club president Clarence Wheeler), Dr. Williams started a nursery in the backyard of his home at 388 Monroe Avenue. He purchased thousands of seedlings and also used seedlings mailed to him free of charge by arborists from all segments of the globe. Some notable acquisitions came from acorns originally planted by George Washington at Mount Vernon, from the Shakespeare Oak at Stratford-upon-Avon, from Sherwood Forest, from the Cedars of Lebanon and from the Kew Gardens of England.

Many of the plants began their lives in neatly lined rows of coffee cans at Williams's home before being nurtured to maturity and then transplanted onto the grounds of Oak Hill. Other trees were planted in non-playing areas around the two courses that served as de facto laboratory forests, and once they blossomed and were ready to live on their own, they were moved to planned-out sections on the courses. "Dr. Williams was certainly one of our most legendary members, and if you looked over the first one hundred years of our history, you would have to say that no one played a greater role in the development of Oak Hill," said Reeves.

Dr. Williams, erudite and regal in his medical office or in the clubhouse at Oak Hill, could often be seen walking the acreage in muddy overalls and boots looking every bit like a grounds crew laborer instead of Oak Hill's most important man. Indeed, it was a labor of love. He once said, "The Almighty was the greatest landscape architect of all. It was His plan to have oaks at Oak Hill." But it was Dr. Williams who implemented that plan. It is estimated that he planted between thirty thousand and forty thousand seedlings, and as you walk the grounds of Oak Hill today, you can't help but gaze at the majestic green mansions that soar to the heavens, lending at once an unmatched beauty and a treacherous detriment to one's scorecard. It boggles the mind to think that nearly all of these wonders began as little acorns in Dr. Williams's backyard garden.

After he died in April 1966 at the age of eighty-nine, Dr. Williams's memory was honored with the dedication of a fountain located prominently beside the paths leading to both the East and West Courses. Martin Gullen, who succeeded Dr. Williams and preceded Reeves as the Hill of Fame chairman, remarked that it was a "fountain of beauty" dedicated to a "man of vision." The inscription accurately captures the essence of what he meant to Oak Hill:

*To John R. Williams—whose vision, loyalty and devotion have transformed homely farmland into a country club estate of unsurpassed beauty, his fellow club members join in doing honor. As this boulder has come down through the ages, so shall the ever-increasing charm and witchery of this Oak Hill scene bear witness to the realization of his dreams.*

*Chapter 6*

# Time to Show Off

In only a few years, it became clear that the combination of Ross's design and Dr. Williams's arboreal augmentation had created a soon-to-be masterpiece, and it was time to put the more brutish and tournament-worthy East Course to the test. In 1934, as a dual celebration of Rochester's centennial and the twentieth anniversary of native son Walter Hagen's first U.S. Open triumph, the Walter Hagen Centennial Open was contested. With some of the era's finest professional golfers on hand offering their praise for a layout still in its infancy, Oak Hill cast its first footprint on the national scene.

The centennial was a noble reason to hold a golf tournament, but let's make no mistake about it—Hagen was the centerpiece, the drawing card. During his two decades at or near the top of the burgeoning world of golf, Hagen enjoyed international fame, and the city pounded its collective chest with pride all eleven times he won a major golf championship.

Born in Rochester in 1892, Hagen, the only male among five siblings, grew up in Corbett's Glen near Brighton, where his father was a blacksmith. He discovered golf as a young boy, playing the game in the family cow pasture. Hagen would herd the bovine into spots where he had dug holes so that they could munch on the grass and create better conditions for putting. Given his interest in the game, he sought work as a caddie at the newly incorporated Country Club of Rochester, learning invaluable lessons about golf—and life—from the club pro, Andy Christy. Hagen quickly became proficient, and when he was given the opportunity to play, he was beating far more experienced men rather easily. He was also a fine baseball player, and as a teenager, he often

Walter Hagen putting at the thirteenth green during the Walter Hagen Centennial in 1934.

contemplated a career in the Major Leagues. While playing semipro ball for a team in Rochester, he was spotted by a scout from the Philadelphia Phillies of the National League and was offered a tryout in Florida in 1914. Hagen had a previous engagement, though. He had recently declared professional status as a golfer and was entered in the U.S. Open at Midlothian Country Club outside Chicago. At the age of twenty-one, he won the tournament with a score of 290 and took home a check for $300, forever changing his life, as well as the perception of professional golfers.

At that time, amateur tournament-level golfers were considered true competitors—men who played the game for the competition and not for a paycheck—just like ordinary members of golf clubs. Professionals were considered play-for-pay miscreants and were treated as such. When they arrived to play open events, they weren't allowed inside the locker room like the amateurs. They were forced to dress in pro shops, restrooms or their own automobiles if need be. If they were hungry or thirsty, they were on their own because they were prohibited from entering the clubhouse.

Hagen, who had a habit of arriving just minutes before his start time, dressing in his car and running to the first tee (often with booze on his

Leo Diegel won the Walter Hagen Centennial with an eight-under-par total of 276.

breath after a night out on the town), railed against these injustices and ultimately broke down the barriers for professionals. His tremendous skill and success, combined with his handsome visage, engaging personality and natty attire, made him a role model—someone amateur golfers wanted to emulate.

They also could do nothing but marvel at the man's talent. On his way to becoming the first professional athlete in any sport to earn $1 million, Hagen's eleven major tournament victories (two U.S. Opens, four British Opens and five PGA Championships, the last coming in 1929) stood as the career standard until 1973, when Jack Nicklaus won the PGA Championship at Canterbury for the twelfth of his record eighteen major titles. Tiger Woods, with fourteen majors, also now ranks ahead of Hagen, but none of the other greats, such as Bobby Jones, Ben Hogan, Byron Nelson, Arnold Palmer, Lee Trevino or Tom Watson, ever equaled or surpassed "The Haig."

Through the years, as professional golfers enjoyed more and more hospitality and respect (not to mention bigger purses), the greatest names in the game routinely paid homage to Hagen. "Without you, golf would not be what it is today. I give you my deepest thanks," said Hogan. From Nelson: "There is absolutely no way that we golf professionals can properly thank you for your great contribution to our profession." And from Gene Sarazen: "All the professionals who have the chance to go after the big money today should say a silent prayer to Walter Hagen. It was Walter who made professional golf what it is."

Of course, there were many who just found Hagen to be a laugh riot—which he was. One time, while playing golf in Great Britain with Edward, Duke of Windsor, the carefree Haig had the temerity to say, "Hey Eddie, hold the flag, would you please." A gallery filled with Brits gasped at the suggestion, but the duke gladly did so and said later of Hagen, "I recall the great kick we all used to get out of watching him play and win on the great championship courses." Comedian, entertainer and avid golfer Bob Hope once said after playing with Hagen, "Walter's the fellow who said, 'After watching Bob's swing, you're not sure which restroom he uses.'"

When Oak Hill announced that it was honoring Rochester's hometown hero by hosting the first prominent tournament at its relatively new home in Pittsford, many of the best players in the world from both the professional and amateur ranks flocked to town to celebrate Hagen's career. Leo Diegel, who would ultimately win the seventy-two-hole event with a dazzling score of eight-under-par (276), was joined by, among others, Ky Laffoon, Harry Cooper, Paul Runyan, Joe Turnesa, Olin Dutra, Denny Shute and Ed Dudley. Hagen, whose playing days were mostly behind him, finished twelve strokes behind Diegel.

Diegel was the man who ended Hagen's four-year reign at the PGA Championship when he won in 1928 and '29. He had also played on America's first four Ryder Cup teams—all captained by Hagen—so his victory at Oak Hill seemed quite appropriate. He opened with 70-69, and playing the last thirty-six holes on the same day, he put up 71 in the morning and then a stunning five-birdie, no-bogey 66 in the afternoon to defeat Laffoon by two shots. "Rochester put over a great tournament, and I hope to see it become a yearly fixture," said Bob Harlow, who was formerly Hagen's manager and the future founder of *Golf World* magazine.

Unfortunately, that did not happen, and golf's greatest players did not return to Oak Hill until the *Times-Union* newspaper sponsored tournaments in 1941 and '42. Another star-studded cast, now drawn solely by the rapidly maturing East Course and a $5,000 purse put up by newspaper publisher and Oak Hill member Frank Gannett, descended on Oak Hill for the first Times-Union Open. Stars included Hogan, Sarazen, Runyan, Shute, Sam Snead, Craig

Publisher and Oak Hill member Frank Gannett, who founded Gannett News Service and set up its flagship in Rochester, passes out prize checks to Craig Wood (left), Ben Hogan (middle) and Sam Snead (right) following the 1941 Times-Union Open.

Wood, Jug McSpaden, Ray Mangrum, Clayton Heafner, Johnny Bulla, Horton Smith, Lloyd Mangrum, Mike Turnesa and Bobby Cruickshank. There was plenty of local flavor in the mix as well. Irondequoit head pro Frank Commisso thrilled his legions by finishing tied for eleventh with a 291 total. Dr. George Trainor, who was then a member at Monroe but would soon join Oak Hill and ultimately win the club championship five times, was low amateur at 301. Jack Mooney was the low Oak Hill scorer at 317, while Bill Chapin, who would begin a string of four straight Oak Hill club championships in 1941, was the only other Oak Hill player to make the cut, finishing at 323.

By playing the seventeenth hole as a long par-four instead of the members' short par-five—a tradition that would continue whenever a major tournament was played at Oak Hill—the East Course played as a par 70. Snead began with a fine 67 and led hometown hero Commisso by two strokes, as they were the only two players in the 138-man field to break par. While Commisso skied to a 76 on the second day, Snead tacked on a 70 to lead Wood by three shots. But in the third round, Snead encountered some difficulty of his own and struggled to a 73. That allowed Wood, winner of the 1941 Masters and U.S. Open, to grab a one-shot advantage on the strength of a well-earned 69.

Ben Hogan watches a tee shot during the first round of the 1942 Times-Union, during which he set a competitive course record of 64 that remains unbroken to this day.

Wood—who was such a good friend of Claude Harmon that he became the namesake of Harmon's second son, Craig Wood Harmon, the head professional at Oak Hill the past four decades—endured a rough afternoon, though. He carded six bogeys and a double-bogey at the eighteenth hole for an unruly 78, dropping him to third place. Meanwhile, Snead recaptured his first-round magic and signed for another 67, giving him a three-under-par 277 total, seven shots better than Hogan, whose final-round 67 bumped him up to second place at 284. Snead set a back nine East Course record with a 32 as he birdied holes ten, thirteen and sixteen to run away from the pack as a gallery estimated at six thousand roared its approval.

Hogan, so impressed by Oak Hill, promised to return if the event was held in 1942. It was, and he did—and it was his show from start to finish. Just twenty-nine at the time and without a major victory on his resume, the fierce Texan opened with a 64 that included a double-bogey on the seventeenth hole. More than seventy years have passed, and that is still a record score on the East Course, having been tied only by Curtis Strange in the second round of the 1989 U.S. Open and by Rochester's own Jeff Sluman, who posted that number in 1985 during a non-tournament round played with friends.

The field in 1942 was much the same as it was in '41. Hogan, Wood, McSpaden, Laffoon, Smith, Turnesa, Sarazen and Cruickshank all showed up, and Jimmy Demaret and Ralph Guldahl made their Oak Hill debuts. Two notable absentees were defending champion Snead, who was off serving in the military, and Byron Nelson, who had also missed the '41 tournament. But it really didn't matter who was or wasn't there because Hogan led from start to finish. After middle rounds of 68 and 72, he entered the fourth round with a five-stroke cushion, and intermittent rain and tricky winds guaranteed that no one was going to make a move on him. He three-putted holes three and eight to make bogeys, and then he bogeyed seventeen and eighteen to close out an uninspiring 74, which was still three better than Wood.

*Chapter 7*

# Where Have You Been?

There's a tree that stands regally near the thirteenth green of the East Course that is dedicated, as part of the Hill of Fame, to Joseph Dey, one of the most influential golf administrators in the history of the game. Dey, a highly skilled amateur player from Norfolk, Virginia, grew up in New Orleans and worked as a sportswriter in Philadelphia before joining the United States Golf Association (USGA) in 1930. Starting in 1934, Dey served as the organization's executive director until 1968, and during his tenure, he helped shepherd golf through a period of exponential change and growth.

It was Dey who served as the key American figure when the USGA and the Royal and Ancient Golf Club at St. Andrews (the governing body of the sport in Europe) met in 1951 to synchronize the Official Rules of Golf. Dey also oversaw the selection of USGA tournament sites and the setup of those courses for championship play; he helped inaugurate five new USGA championships, including the U.S. Women's Open; and he gave the blessing for the building of the USGA Museum and Library. After leaving the USGA, he served as commissioner of the PGA Tour (then known as the Tournament Players Division of the PGA) during the tumultuous period when the players broke away from the PGA of America until Deane Beman took the reins in 1974.

If ever there was a man who embodied the spirit and the requisites of the Hill of Fame, it was Dey. However, even if Dey had none of those impressive credentials on his resume, he may have been deemed Hill of Fame worthy

Charlie Coe of Oklahoma won two U.S. Amateur titles and was one of America's greatest amateur players.

by the Oak Hill membership for a simple yet powerful and history-altering comment he made during a visit to Oak Hill in 1948 while he was scouting potential sites for the 1949 U.S. Amateur Open. "Where have you been for twenty years?" Dey asked. "There's nothing like this in the whole country." And just like that, Oak Hill was awarded the Amateur. A year later, when it conducted a fabulously successful tournament witnessed by more than fifteen thousand fans and won by Oklahoman Charlie Coe, Oak Hill's destiny as a major championship host was consummated.

Former USGA president William Campbell, who played in the 1949 Amateur and was one of America's foremost amateurs before ascending the ranks of the USGA, once said of Dey, "In the world of golf, Joe Dey was the mightiest oak of all." Quite an apt and appropriate description of a man who played such a key role in the establishment of Oak Hill's credentials.

During the week that bridged late August with early September, Campbell reached the match-play semifinals, but there he ran into the rail-thin Coe and was buzz-sawed into submission, 8 and 7. The next day, Coe pummeled Texan Rufus King by 11 and 10 in what was scheduled to be a thirty-six-hole championship match that ended after a mere twenty-six holes, still the second most lopsided final in the tournament's 113-year history. "Naturally, your first major championship is special," said Coe in an interview late in his life before passing away in 2001 at the age of 77.

Coe is regarded as one of the best amateur players to ever call the United States home—at least that's what Jack Nicklaus thinks. "Charlie Coe was a good player—I don't think there's any question about that," said Nicklaus, who at the age of nineteen defeated Coe 1-up in the 1959 Amateur at the Broadmoor Golf Club in Colorado Springs, signaling to the golf world

Sam Urzetta, the pride of East Rochester, who would win the 1950 U.S. Amateur in Minneapolis, lost his first-round match at Oak Hill in the 1949 tournament.

what was to come for the next few decades. "Charlie finished second in the Masters in '61, and he was always competitive in any event he ever played in. Charlie was just a good, solid player. I don't think Charlie was a spectacular player like some of the guys are today, but he always got the job done."

Rochester's Sam Urzetta, who won the 1950 U.S. Amateur at Minneapolis Golf Club and later served nearly four decades as the head professional at the Country Club of Rochester, recalled Coe as a "great competitor. He was marvelous. He had a great short game and he was a good match play player. I think his record speaks for itself."

Coe could have turned pro and competed against the best of the best, recalling, "My wife said if I wanted to do that, it was fine with her." Of course, if he did, then he wouldn't be married to her. So he made a nice living in the oil business and continued on the amateur circuit. He went on to win the 1958 Amateur at the Olympic Club in San Francisco and played on six Walker Cup teams, putting together a record of 7-4-2 before captaining the victorious 1959 U.S. Walker Cup team.

When he occasionally tested himself against the pros, Coe lent credence to the belief that he could have survived quite nicely among their ranks. He tied for thirteenth in the 1958 U.S. Open at Southern Hills and tied for thirty-eighth at the '59 Open at Winged Foot, but it was at the Masters where Coe established his legacy. He holds the amateur records for most starts (nineteen), most cuts made (fifteen), most rounds played (sixty-seven), most rounds at par or better (twenty-two), most top-ten finishes (three), most times low amateur (six) and lowest seventy-two-hole score (281). That seven-under-par total was produced in 1961, the year he finished tied for second with Arnold Palmer behind winner Gary Player.

"I'm very proud of my amateur status," said Coe.

When the players began arriving at Oak Hill from all corners of the country, Coe was merely an afterthought, despite the fact that the week before, he had won his singles match to help the United States to a 10–2 drubbing of Great Britain and Ireland in the Walker Cup matches at Winged Foot.

Willie Turnesa, who had won his second amateur title the year before, was the odds-on favorite at Oak Hill, and it was expected that fellow Walker Cup teammates Skee Riegel (1947 Amateur champ), Ted Bishop (1946 champ), Ray Billows (three-time runner-up and a seven-time New York State champion who had won one of those titles at Oak Hill in 1945), John Dawson and Frank Stranahan would be heard from. Harvie Ward, the son of two-time Amateur champion Marvin H. Ward, who would go on to match his father's feat by winning this title in 1955 and '56, let it be known that he was ready for battle as he tied the East Course amateur record with a 66 during a practice round.

Also in the field were future USGA officials Campbell and P.J. Boatwright, as well as Ben Hogan's older brother, Royal Hogan. There was also a talented contingent of youngsters who would ultimately achieve great success as professionals: nineteen-year-old Palmer, Julius Boros, Dow Finsterwald and Gay Brewer. And of course, there was the pride of East Rochester, Urzetta, winner of the 1948 New York State Amateur about whom PGA pro and future fellow Hill of Fame member Chick Evans said before the tournament began: "His tee shots are fine, especially that little fade of his, and he's a fine putter." Urzetta would reward Evans's faith a year later when he defeated Stranahan on the thirty-ninth hole of the Amateur championship in Minneapolis.

But there was no one who could touch Coe during this week. "I didn't feel like I was sneaking up on anybody," Coe recalled. "I didn't have any wild ideas about winning the tournament at any point. I came to play."

Urzetta was naturally the fan favorite, but he and the other locals in the field—Oak Hill head pro Charlie McKenna's son Charlie Jr., Oak Hill member Bobby Hill, Monroe Golf Club's Mort Reed, Brook-Lea Country Club's Cliff Goodrich and Ray Allen from the Country Club of Rochester—were all eliminated by the time the third round was complete.

Coe was given a first-round bye and then swung into action on the second day with a 4-and-3 romp over C.T. Garth Jr. Coe was simply brilliant on day three, as he won the first six holes of his 8-and-7 morning romp over Louis Wendrow and then cruised to a 4-and-2 victory over Bob Sweeny to advance to the round of sixteen. But by the time the wind-blown fourth day of competition was finished, Coe wasn't sure he'd have enough energy to finish the grueling tournament, as both of his matches went into overtime. "I'm really tired, and I mean really tired," the 140-pound Coe drawled after eliminating Ward on the nineteenth and Dawson on the twenty-first. "You know, I played forty holes today, and every one of them was tough. I was sure lucky to beat Mr. Dawson—just plain lucky."

Coe was 3-down with five to play against Ward but rallied to win holes fourteen, fifteen and sixteen to get square. They halved seventeen and eighteen, and then Coe won with a birdie on the first extra hole. Against Dawson, it went the other way. Coe was 2-up through twelve, but Dawson won thirteen and fourteen and had a chance to put the match away at eighteen. Coe pulled his drive into the rough and was just off the green in three, while Dawson hit an iron that left him dancing sixty feet from the cup in regulation. Coe chipped to within "gimme" range for a bogey. Then Dawson three-putted, and Coe was spared. Both players parred the next two holes, and when Dawson lipped out a two-footer for bogey at hole three, the match was over. "That's what kind of started the tournament for me," Coe said. "I don't remember the first two or three matches, but I remember that day."

In the semifinals, Turnesa lost a shocker to King, 2 and 1, and Coe steamrolled Campbell, 8 and 7. "If he [King] continues his fine play," Turnesa said, "he and Charlie Coe should have a great match."

Well, not so much. Coe was on an unstoppable roll. Against Campbell, he was 4-up after the morning eighteen, and then Campbell imploded with two double-bogeys and a bogey on the first three holes in the afternoon to drop hopelessly out of contention. "I was just plain lousy," Campbell summarized. To which Coe replied, "Well, let's just say I've been scrambling pretty good."

Coe was known to be a bit modest, and the reality was that this man, whose swing was so fluid that Byron Nelson once said, "That's the way I try to look when I swing," did everything good at Oak Hill. When his evisceration of King was complete, Coe said humbly, "I don't think I'm the number-one amateur in the nation just because I've won. But although I was fortunate enough to win, I'm not afraid of any amateur in the country."

More than three thousand fans strode along with Coe and King on a radiant day, the rain and cold and wind that had plagued some of the tournament's early rounds a mere memory. Both players began boorishly as

Charlie Coe is congratulated by Dr. John R. Williams following his victory over Rufus King.

each bogeyed the first two holes, then King's bogey at hole three was good enough to beat Coe's double-bogey for a 1-up lead. That would be the only hole Coe would lose all day. He regrouped quickly and won hole four with a birdie. Then, after halving five and six with pars, King hit a dreadful stretch wherein he bogeyed four in a row, and Coe won all four holes with pars to take a commanding lead.

When they broke for lunch, King was 5-down after making a bogey at eighteen, and when the players returned to the course, King's luck didn't change. Coe won the first five holes (three with birdies) to go 10-up and then closed the match with a stylish birdie on the twenty-sixth. "I was mighty lucky," Coe said. Not so, according to King, who remarked, "He was too good. I couldn't have beaten him today no matter what I did. I've got to be honest—the outcome wasn't entirely unexpected so far as I'm concerned."

Coe took home the Havemeyer Trophy, and Oak Hill bathed in the warm press clippings it received from the nation's golf press. Herb Graffis, who founded *Golf* magazine and covered the '49 Amateur, wrote, "There's never been a club to conduct a national tournament any better or more hospitable than Oak Hill. President Otto A. Shults and vice-chairmen of the Amateur championship committee William C. Chapin and James W. Weldon and their teammates were perfect hosts."

The USGA wholeheartedly agreed, as president Fielding Wallace said, "It is my considered opinion that this was one of the most successful, interesting and exciting tournaments ever held."

# Chapter 8
# HILL OF FAME

There may be more picturesque or peaceful places on this earth, but for Bill Reeves, it's tough to top the natural amphitheater that surrounds the thirteenth green of the East Course, which is home to the Hill of Fame, perhaps Oak Hill's most treasured tradition. "There's really something mystical about the place, particularly when you walk down the north side and read the plaques on those trees," said Reeves, who joined Oak Hill in 1949 and took over the chairmanship of the Hill of Fame committee in 1980. "Go out there late in the afternoon and read the plaques, look back at the clubhouse, look out over the East Course, and you'll see something very special."

Half a millennium ago, belying its twenty-first-century serenity, this revered strip of land served as a warring ground for the hostile Indian tribes of the Mohawks, Oneidas, Senecas, Cayugas and Onondagas, who fought bloody territorial battles until the peace-keeping League of the Iroquois was formed. Today, all you hear are birds chirping, gentle breezes rustling through the majestic trees and the occasional yelps of golfers celebrating a well-executed shot or lamenting a poorly played stroke.

Given its combination of legacy and loveliness, the Hill is ideally suited to house the ring of trees where Oak Hill honors, in the words of former Hill chairman Martin Gullen, "the immortals of golf and the distinguished citizens who have enriched the American way of life."

Founded in 1956 by Dr. Williams, defined by Gullen and for more than four decades nurtured by Reeves and a committee composed of past Oak

Hill presidents, the Hill of Fame represents the spirit of Oak Hill and characterizes the importance the club attaches to its history. "I think one of the unique things about Oak Hill—and I hope we never lose it—is that history and tradition really matter here," said Reeves. "A lot of clubs talk about it, but here it really counts. It's interesting to observe new members when they come into the club. At first, people are attracted here by our great golf courses and the wonderful physical amenities that we have, but after a while, people become aware of the great history and traditions that we have here. And those things begin to take on a greater importance to members after they've been here for a while."

In formulating his plan for the Hill of Fame, Dr. Williams decreed that "a living tree is a much better monument than a piece of granite." Not surprising when you consider that it was Dr. Williams who devoted more than half of his life to beautifying the grounds. "The Hill of Fame is really a golf Hall of Fame. But the unique thing about it is that a living thing, a tree, is used as the memorial to the honorees," said Reeves.

Gullen once said, "We look on the Hill of Fame as an institution where men and women may be honored for their fine qualities of heart and mind

The Hill of Fame plaque dedicated to Jack Nicklaus, Arnold Palmer and Gary Player, all of whom played a "Big Three" exhibition match at Oak Hill in 1965.

Bill Reeves, a member at Oak Hill since 1949, has been the chairman of the Hill of Fame for more than thirty years.

and their personal contributions to some phase of human welfare and uplift." And as you scan down the eclectic list of honorees, those attributes chime loudly.

Ranging from Ben Hogan and Rochester's own Walter Hagen to Jack Nicklaus and Curtis Strange; from architects Donald Ross and Robert Trent Jones to past United States Golf Association officials Joseph Dey and James Hand; from former United States presidents Dwight Eisenhower and Gerald Ford to comedian Bob Hope; from amateurs such as Rochester legends Don Allen and Sam Urzetta to female stars such as Nancy Lopez and Babe Didrikson Zaharias; the common bond these people share is their love of the game and their willingness to advance it. "They are an outstanding cross section of people," said Reeves. "I think of it in three sections or categories: the great players, the golf administrators and architects and 'the distinguished citizens who have enriched the American way of life,' to use Marty's words."

Not a round on the East Course passes that Reeves doesn't arrive at the thirteenth green to stop and look around at the splendor of the Hill of Fame. And whenever he's playing host to a guest, a journey around the hill is a prerequisite. "I like to pause momentarily when we get to the Hill of Fame and look around, and almost always at the end of a round, we'll go to the Hill of Fame and look at the trees and plaques," said Reeves. "For most people, it's a very special experience. It recalls the history of the game, the great people who have been in the game and people who have made the game what it is in America. The Hill of Fame is very special to me because it's very special to Oak Hill."

Don Knott, the former president of the American Society of Golf Course Architects who accepted Donald Ross's honor at his 1994 induction, summed up perfectly the intentions of the Hill of Fame when he said:

> *His courses, like this tree, are and will continue to be a pleasure to behold; changing with the seasons; maturing with years; each with its own special characteristics and unique style. Oak Hill is among his finest creations, and in this oak tree, his spirit will continue to live and will surely take great pride and pleasure as it watches over golfers of the day.*

*Chapter 9*

# THE GOOD DOCTOR

Given its rave reviews for its hosting of the Amateur, and armed with the solid backing of men like Fielding Wallace and Joseph Dey, who were clearly enamored with the East Course's fair but bedeviling challenges, it was no surprise when the USGA announced that it was bringing its most prestigious championship, the U.S. Open, to Pittsford in 1956.

In a letter to the membership, Bill Chapin, then club president, wrote, "Only the classic golf courses of the country have been selected in the past to entertain the U.S. Open championship. Now Oak Hill joins this select circle, and we feel certain that when the championship is finally in progress, as well as when it is completed, each member will feel that much greater pride in the membership he holds."

The Open had never been contested in New York anywhere but downstate in Westchester County and on Long Island, and local officials proclaimed that this would be the most prestigious sporting event ever held in this region. And with a star-studded field that included eventual winner Dr. Cary Middlecoff, Ben Hogan, Sam Snead, Arnold Palmer, Gene Littler, Billy Casper, Ken Venturi, Gay Brewer, Dave Marr, Julius Boros, Jimmy Demaret, Chick Harbert, Tommy Bolt and Gardner Dickinson, they were correct.

Although it loved the East Course, the USGA sought some minor alterations to Donald Ross's original layout, so Oak Hill brought in East Rochester's own Robert Trent Jones Sr., one of the most esteemed golf course architects in history, to modernize Ross's work before the Open—a task he had performed at Oakland Hills before the '51 Open and at Baltusrol in '54.

Hogan, so complimentary of the East Course fourteen years earlier when he won the Times-Union Open, was not as impressed upon his return and said during a practice round, "This is the easiest course I've ever seen for a national Open." But Hogan probably wasn't feeling that way by the end of the week when he missed a thirty-inch putt on the seventy-first hole that played a pivotal role in Middlecoff's one-stroke victory, thus preventing him from winning his fifth Open title (which would have made him the new career leader).

Hogan had been on a quest for the record-breaking Open triumph since 1953, when he won at Oakmont to join fellow four-time winners Willie Anderson and Bobby Jones. In 1955 at Olympic, he had the mark dead in his steely-eyed sights until a relative unknown named Jack Fleck birdied the seventy-second hole to tie him and then stunned the world by defeating the icon in an eighteen-hole playoff the next day. Hogan worked himself into position at Oak Hill, and the large galleries that lined the fairways and encircled the greens were roaring with every stroke, hoping to witness history. But Hogan was derailed at the end by his own rather stunning miss—and by a superbly clutch make by Middlecoff. "I would say that was the greatest accomplishment I ever had on one particular, very important shot," Middlecoff said a few years before his death in 1998 of the four-foot downhill slider for par that ultimately secured his second Open title. "That was the big shot of the tournament for me. I knew I was going to win if I could make it."

Still, while it's certainly not fair to Middlecoff, it was Hogan's yip that left an indelible stamp on Oak Hill's inaugural foray into major championship golf. While some fans and players congratulated Middlecoff for winning, most spent their time consoling Hogan for losing. "It hit the hole and stayed out," said Middlecoff, who had finished nearly an hour earlier and was in the locker room watching on television. "I appreciated that."

Appreciated is exactly what Middlecoff's victory often is not. So much of the post-tournament talk was centered on Hogan, but the real story was Middlecoff and his numbing consistency during the four days of competition. He never broke the East Course's par 70—established for the tournament by turning the members' par-five seventeenth into a par-four—but his rounds of 71-70-70-70 could not be matched. And by rolling in that tricky par putt at the end, he afforded himself the opportunity to hoist the championship trophy just as he had done at Medinah in 1949. "The 1956 Open was the

*Left*: Arnold Palmer stares down an approach shot during the 1956 U.S. Open.

*Below*: From left are Sam Snead, Ed Furgol and Lew Worsham at the 1956 U.S. Open.

more satisfying of the two," Middlecoff said. "When I won in 1949, I didn't realize how important it was."

Born in Halls, Tennessee, in 1921, Middlecoff became interested in golf as a youngster. He won the Memphis city championship and Tennessee State Amateur while still a teenager, and during his collegiate career at the University of Mississippi, he won a tournament by a whopping twenty-nine strokes. In 1945, playing in the final group with star pros Hogan and Gene Sarazen, Middlecoff became the first amateur to win the North & South Open, and Bobby Jones was moved to say, "I'd give the world to have a swing like that."

Middlecoff majored in dentistry and upon graduation perfected that skill while serving eighteen months in the Dental Corps during World War II. When his military hitch was up, he mapped out a two-year plan for a career in pro golf. If within those two years he hadn't enjoyed any success, he would return to dentistry. "The fact that I had that dental degree…I knew I wasn't going to starve," Middlecoff said. "I almost went broke a couple times, and I thought, 'You dumb jerk, why don't you go back?'"

Instead, Middlecoff persevered. He won the Charlotte Open in 1947 as a rookie and then began the '49 season by winning three of the first five tournaments on the schedule and finishing runner-up in the other two. When he won the Open, a wire service story proclaimed, "Golf's long search for a new star may be ended."

Middlecoff, who was known for his deliberate style of play, went on to win forty PGA Tour events, which still ranks him tenth all-time. In addition to his two Open crowns, he captured the 1955 Masters and played on three Ryder Cup teams before retiring after 1961 to start what became a twenty-year career as a television golf analyst.

The old joke on tour was that the reason Middlecoff gave up dentistry was because his patients couldn't hold their mouths open that long. But it was his attention to detail that keyed his success, and never was that more evident than on that four-footer on Oak Hill's eighteenth green.

Hogan, bemoaning the tattered state of his game, opened with a 72, which left him four strokes behind Bob Rosburg, who made sixteen pars and two birdies using his unique baseball-style grip. Middlecoff shot a 71. Australian Peter Thomson, the two-time defending British Open champion who stood alone in second place with a first-round 70, followed with a 69 to assume the thirty-six-hole lead, his 139 total one better than Hogan, who fashioned a superb 68 in oppressively warm, windless conditions. Middlecoff, who had a triple-bogey seven on the seventeenth, came in with a 70 to reside tied for

Ben Hogan waits for the group in front to clear the fairway.

third at 141 with Wesley Ellis, Ed Furgol and Jerry Barber. "I think I just blew the Open," Middlecoff said to his caddie, Bill Anson, after the disaster on seventeen.

The early week heat gave way to an overcast and cool Saturday, good news in an era in which the final thirty-six holes were played on the same day. With Hogan in contention, the scene around the course was electric, and Hogan stayed in touch with a morning third-round 72 that left him one back of the new leader, Middlecoff, who stood at 211. Because the USGA didn't re-pair for the afternoon fourth round or pay heed to who was leading, the players were sent off haphazardly, and Middlecoff teed off somewhere in the middle of the pack. This would set the stage for an odd finish to the tournament, as Middlecoff would post his 281 total almost two hours before the last golfers had concluded play.

Middlecoff played the afternoon front nine even. He dumped his approach at ten into a bunker but splashed out to within five feet and saved par. At twelve, he missed the green to the right but chipped to three feet and salvaged another par. At the thirteenth, he drained a twenty-five-footer for birdie, and when he rolled in a twelve-footer for birdie at fourteen, it looked as if he would coast to the championship. But after a par at fifteen, he was confronted with the East Course's grueling closing holes, and he barely survived. "They sure were tough," he said, referring to his abysmal eight-over-par performance on those three holes during the championship. "I almost fell dead at the last three holes. I made five on sixteen and five on seventeen—that apple jumped up in my throat and almost choked me."

Middlecoff drove into the rough at sixteen, bunkered his approach and then lipped out a seven-footer for par to give back a stroke. At seventeen, he chunked his second shot into the gallery on the left and eventually missed a twelve-footer for par. "I hit good drives on both holes, and after the bogeys, I was about ready to give up," he said. "I was just hoping for a playoff then."

But even a playoff looked like a reach when he hooked his drive at eighteen into the gnarly rough on the left, making it impossible for him to reach the green in regulation. "I knew there was no way I could get over that chasm in front of the green, so I played up the left rough purposely," Middlecoff explained. "That particular year, the rough was not really severe because they'd had a late spring." From that position, he chipped adeptly onto the putting surface, and his ball stopped four feet above the hole.

At just about the same time, Hogan dazzled the record crowd with a wedge to within three feet on the fourteenth to set up a birdie that pulled him to within one shot. If Middlecoff didn't make his putt, his lead would be evaporated, so he went to work the way only Middlecoff could. "I wandered around and found the old cup about twenty feet behind the hole, almost on the same line," he recalled. "I remembered in the practice round I putted the putt several times the way it looked it should go—and missed. I kept looking up and down, and it still didn't look like it was going to go the way it did. I said to myself, 'You stood here last Wednesday and missed it three or four times.' That was one of the hardest things I ever did, talking myself into putting it against the way it looked like it would break."

Middlecoff knocked it into the heart of the cup and nearly melted in relief. Now began the arduous task of waiting for the contenders to finish. Hogan was first, and in between narrowly missing birdie putts at sixteen and eighteen came the stunning miss at seventeen. "Seventeen is tough, yes. But it wasn't the toughness of the hole that got me; it was the missed putt," Hogan said. "I hit the ball badly. You shouldn't win when you miss like that."

When Boros failed to make a birdie in the last four holes and Ted Kroll made triple bogey at sixteen, Middlecoff could finally breathe a sigh of relief, knowing that as a two-time winner of the Open, his name would now

Dr. Cary Middlecoff poses with the U.S. Open trophy.

become synonymous with greatness. "They don't remember who won the weekly tournaments, but they remember the Open," he said. "And as big and as fine as the Masters is, the Open is still the biggest. It has the name of your country on it. Nobody wins the Open—it wins you."

*Chapter 10*

# BREAKTHROUGH FOR THE "MERRY MEX"

There were the long birdie putts at the eleventh and twelfth holes during the final round that helped Lee Trevino take control of the 1968 Open. "Yeah, those were nice," Trevino said. There was the nervous feeling of walking up to the eighteenth green, four shots ahead of Jack Nicklaus, knowing that he was on the verge of winning not only his first major championship but also his first PGA Tour event. "I was so nervous, I couldn't get my shots airborne," Trevino said, laughing at the memory. "If you look at the tape, all my shots were low drives. I was choking so bad."

But that wasn't the recollection that rings loudest when Trevino thinks back to that momentous day at Oak Hill when he announced to the world his arrival as a professional golfer. "The highlight of that week was meeting Arnold Palmer for the first time," said the man who used Oak Hill as the launching point to one of the most successful and entertaining careers in PGA history. "I remember sitting in the tent and signing my card. I won, but Arnold got a bigger ovation than I did. He came over, shook my hand and said, 'Nice going, young man.' I had never met him before. Man, that was something."

And Trevino was sure something that week at Oak Hill, as he became the first player in the sixty-eight-year history of the U.S. Open to break par in every round, his five-under-par total of 275 tying the Open record set just a year earlier in 1967 at Baltusrol by Nicklaus.

At a time when Palmer had already begun his descent from the lofty perch where he ruled the golf world in the late 1950s and early 1960s, Trevino

Lee Trevino chips as a portion of the periscope-toting gallery looks on.

burst onto the scene with this victory. His out-of-nowhere domination of the East Course kick-started a career that included another Open triumph (1971), two British Open victories (1971 and '72), two PGA Championship victories (1974 and 1984), twenty-nine total PGA Tour victories and twenty-nine Champions Tour victories. "Oak Hill was where I won my first tournament," Trevino said. "Thank God it was a big one—the U.S. Open."

Trevino joined the tour in 1967, and his sixth-place finish at Baltusrol was his big payday, as it secured his playing privileges for 1968. He won $26,472 as a rookie, was forty-fifth on the money list and *Golf Digest* selected him as its Rookie of the Year.

Nicklaus remembered Trevino's play at the Open, saying, "He had played well in 1967, but I didn't really know him." No one really did, and that didn't change much in 1968, as Trevino didn't do a whole lot in the first half of the season.

A couple weeks before teeing it up at Oak Hill, Trevino had nearly earned his first pro victory in Houston, but he lost a late lead, and Roberto De Vicenzo stole the tournament. "I had been playing well that year, but I blew [the Houston] tournament," said Trevino. "On the way to Rochester, I stopped in Utica and watched some Little League baseball. Then I stopped at McDonald's, got a six-pack of beer, found a motel room and stayed overnight."

Refreshed and feeling ready to go, the "Merry Mex," as he became known, completed the trip to Rochester the next day. And when he showed up at the Pittsford home of Paul and Barbara Kircher, he was greeted by Barbara, who was clad only in a black bathing suit. He knew then that it would be an interesting week. "Now, this is an attractive lady, and I had never stayed with anyone before," Trevino said, laughing at the thought. "She was unpacking groceries, and she had all these cans of Mexican food, so I asked her, 'Do you like Mexican food?' And she said, 'No, I bought it for you.' I said, 'I don't eat that stuff.'"

Paul Kircher recalled how the connection with Trevino came about:

> *Probably three weeks prior to tournament time, I received a phone call from a former business associate who had retired and moved to Dallas and in so doing became a friend of Lee's by practicing at the same driving range Lee frequently used. Subsequently, when Lee qualified for that year's U.S. Open, I received a phone call from him asking me if we'd be interested in housing him. I didn't give it much thought. I said, 'Sure, I'd be glad to.' Lee had no money at the time. He had three pairs of slacks and three shirts that my wife washed every night so he had something to wear. We didn't expect anything that developed. He was just trying to save some money, and we were trying to get closer to the action.*

If it was action they wanted, Trevino certainly provided it. He played his practice rounds with veteran pro Doug Sanders, and Trevino knew the course suited his game. Each day, he got more comfortable with the holes and how they played. He later said, "I just fell in love with the course."

And then Oak Hill and Rochester fell in love with him.

Trevino started with a 69 on a cool, drizzly day and was sitting two strokes behind Bert Yancey. Nicklaus, who predicted before the tournament began that Trevino would be in the hunt, admitted to having difficulty reading the greens and shot 72, while Palmer sniffed about the inconsistent sand in the bunkers (even though it came from his home state of Pennsylvania) and shot a 73.

Yancey continued his solid play in the second round and stayed two strokes ahead of Trevino as they each shot 68, prompting Yancey to boldly proclaim, "Trevino's got to catch me." Trevino was wondering how he'd do it, especially after the way he played on day two, even though that was his best score of the week. "I missed seven or eight fairways and got off with a 68," he said with a noticeable sigh of relief. "I hit the tee ball very badly. You're supposed to bogey when you reach the rough, but my putting saved me."

Nicklaus said he wasn't discouraged after a 70 dropped him seven strokes behind Yancey, but the same could not be said for Palmer. He followed his

Jack Nicklaus failed to defend his 1967 U.S. Open title, as he finished four shots behind winner Lee Trevino.

73 with a sloppy 74, prompting one of his faithful Arnie's Army members to declare, "He stinks." To a certain extent, Palmer agreed, saying, "It was a simple case of atrocious putting. Tomorrow, I may leave the putter in the bag and use my finger to roll the ball up."

Bert Yancey (left), who began the fourth round with a one-shot lead, couldn't hold off Lee Trevino.

It wouldn't have mattered what Palmer used to putt with in the third round. He played abysmally, skying to an embarrassing 79, which sent him plummeting to near the bottom of the pack. "I've tried everything," Palmer said of a slump that had now reached worrisome proportions. "I've tried giving a damn, and I've tried not giving a damn—and it hasn't made any difference."

Meanwhile, Yancey and Trevino further separated themselves from the field with a 70 and 69, respectively, leaving Trevino one shot in arrears heading into the last eighteen. Seven strokes behind Yancey, Nicklaus conceded, "I'd have to shoot 65 or so in order to catch him."

Paul Kircher did not doubt that Nicklaus could shoot 65, but it was his opinion that even if he did, he wasn't going to catch Trevino. He was also pretty sure that Yancey was not going to be able to hold up, so on the eve of the final round, Kircher began preparing for a Trevino victory celebration scheduled for the next night. "I was convinced Lee was going to win," Kircher said. "I had a friend who owned a liquor store. It was after hours, but he went down and opened it up so I could buy some champagne."

Twenty-four hours later, corks were popping, many of Kircher's neighbors in Pittsford decorated their front lawns with congratulatory signs and Trevino was waving around his lone $20 bill with one hand and a USGA-endorsed check for $30,000 in the other. Trevino closed with his third 69 of the week, which was more than enough to hold off the hard-charging 67 of Nicklaus. In a phone call back to his home course in Dallas, Horizon Hills Country Club, Trevino informed club manager Don Whittington to pour "free booze all night for all the members."

Nicklaus made an early charge with birdies at holes three and four and was within three shots of the lead as Yancey bogeyed numbers one and three. Trevino started with a bogey at the first but then parred eight in a row to take a one-stroke lead over Yancey, who played the front three-over.

With victory in sight, Trevino got serious. He stopped his merry bantering with the galleries and waved goodbye to Yancey and Nicklaus with a pair of clutch birdies—a thirty-five-footer at the par-three eleventh and a twenty-footer at the par-four twelfth. Up ahead, Nicklaus was all over the flagstick on every hole, but he couldn't gain any ground because he couldn't make a putt. "I kid you not, I feel that my round out there today is the finest I've ever played in a U.S. Open," Nicklaus said in discussing his 67 that leapfrogged him into second place at one-under 279.

Yet it was all for naught. Trevino parred thirteen, fourteen and fifteen and remembered thinking:

> *I never even thought about winning the tournament until I left the fifteenth hole where I hit the flag with an 8-iron. Then I realized I had a shot at winning the Open because I had a five-stroke lead with three holes to go. And that's when I went into my bad play. I was coughing and leaking oil. I'm certainly glad I didn't think about winning the thing beforehand, I might have had a heart attack.*

That tragedy was averted, thanks in part to another local, eighteen-year-old Kevin Quinn of East Rochester, who worked as Trevino's caddie that week. Trevino later said of Quinn:

> *That kid was great; I couldn't have won it without him. He talked to me all the way around. You'd think I was the caddie and him the pro. I asked him if I could drive it out of bounds on the left at eighteen, and he said no. Then I was in the rough, and I asked him what I should hit, and he said to lay it up and then hit a wedge in. I told him, "Kevin, I don't want to be remembered as the U.S. Open champion who laid up.*

Lee Trevino is all smiles after winning for the first time as a member of the PGA Tour.

Trevino opted for a 6-iron, which missed the green, but he chipped to four feet and made the putt that sealed the deal. "It was an unforgettable week for me," Trevino said. "One of the best things was that no one knew me. I sat in a golf cart one night drinking beer, and not one person asked for an autograph. They thought I was the cart boy or something. Rochester will always have a special place in my memory."

*Chapter 11*

# MUSTACHE ON THE MONA LISA

There are hundreds of Donald Ross–designed courses in the United States, and many of them have been left almost completely intact, except perhaps for some new tees to compensate for the power of today's players and the improvement in equipment. Oak Hill's West Course would be a prime example of this, as would the neighboring Monroe Golf Club a few miles away in Pittsford.

Such is not the case with the East Course. It has retained many of Ross's original principles, but in order to stay relevant and in contention for the hosting of major tournaments, it has had to undergo changes—some favorable, some highly controversial. The first true alterations were implemented by Dr. John Williams with the tree-planting program that transformed Ross's original barren sculpture.

Prior to the 1956 Open, Robert Trent Jones Sr. did some remodeling, the bulk of his work a response to the increased skill of that day's player, as he added length to many of the tees and revamped the bunkering system. Too many of the sand traps were out of play for the longer-hitting players, so Jones strategically repositioned some existing bunkers, eliminated others altogether and built new ones that would increase the difficulty of the course. And then, before the 1968 Open, a new par-three hole was built, and Ross's old par-three sixth hole, located in a congested area around the seventh and ninth tees, was eliminated. It was decided that spectator traffic would be too clogged during championship play, so on the suggestion of Davis Love Jr., who at the time was a touring pro and a good friend of then Oak Hill head

Oak Hill member Bob Hoff was instrumental in the controversial renovations that were made to the East Course in the mid-1970s.

pro Jack Lumpkin, Ross's hole was replaced by a new par-three that became the fifth hole, making the next hole, a solid par-four, the sixth hole.

However, by the mid-1970s, it was apparent that without some serious renovation, the East Course was going to fall out of favor with the USGA and the PGA of America. And if proud Oak Hill members refused to believe that, it was confirmed in 1974 when the club's application to host a late 1970s U.S. Open was rebuffed by the USGA. Afterward, longtime members Bob Hoff and Bill Thaney were tasked with coming up with a plan to get the course up to snuff. "After the '68 Open, it was communicated to us very subtly [by the USGA] that we had some problems here so far as holding other major championships, especially the Open," Hoff recalled. "We couldn't leave it the way it was. It was certainly adequate for member play, but we wanted to still be in the rotation to get major tournaments."

Recalling the new par-three hole in 1968, Hoff said, "It wasn't a home run." So he and Thaney concluded that another new hole should be built, and the board of governors approved the idea, as well as the hiring of George Fazio and his nephew, Tom Fazio, to perform the needed work. "The number-one objective was to do something with that par-three hole,"

Hoff said. "George came in several times, and he'd look at that par-three and just shake his head and say, 'You've got a short, flat piece of ground here—what do you want me to do with it?'"

However, George Fazio had once said, "I've never found a golf course where I couldn't build a new par-three." And sure enough, he found a spot at Oak Hill—one that would restore Ross's original hole routing of a par-four fifth hole and a par-three sixth hole. "One day, we were out on the fourth fairway looking down at the creek where it comes under the bridge, and he said that's where the new hole should go," Hoff recalled.

Fazio's idea was to build the new hole in almost the same area as the original par-three hole—only he would change the direction of the shot by building the green hard by the creek, with the water coming into play in front, on the left of and behind the putting surface, with bailout room to the right. There was one problem, though: this green would be too close to the preceding par-four green, Ross's original fifth hole that was then playing as the sixth. So Fazio proposed moving that green forward so that it, too, would sit perilously close to the creek. "Moving that green got everyone riled up," Hoff said. He recalled the infamous quote uttered by member Burt Kling: "We're putting a mustache on the Mona Lisa."

Fazio also suggested building a new green and pond at fifteen and pulling the green at eighteen forward to the crest of the hill for the dual purpose of making the approach shot much more difficult and providing ample space behind the green for spectator bleachers. "It was a rough ten years for me," said Hoff, who bore much of the brunt of the members' anger after the changes were completed. "I think the overwhelming majority of the membership thought we did a terrible thing moving the fifth green. But we did accomplish our objectives, in my opinion. We got every tournament we went after, and some of them came to us."

A point on which Bill Reeves, who was serving his term as club president when the renovation became a hot issue, agrees with Hoff, adding that Oak Hill would not have achieved the status it now enjoys had it not renovated the course. "There are many Ross courses that have been preserved in their original state, almost as museum pieces," he said. "It would be hard to think of an original Ross design that would be suitable for major championship play [now]. I believe that without [the renovation], we would not have had the 1980 PGA and the other major events that followed."

That is certainly true, though it took some time for that reality to sink in. And it did not help when some of the professionals who arrived for the 1980 PGA Championship voiced their displeasure. "Donald Ross is the greatest

George Fazio (hat) and his nephew, Tom Fazio, at the overhauled fifth hole. Tom Fazio was later hired to perform more renovations at Oak Hill.

golf course designer the world has ever known. Why change him?" Joe Inman said. "What is George Fazio thinking when he designs these holes? It takes no talent to make a course tough."

Even Lee Trevino, winner of the 1968 Open who adored the East Course, was disappointed. "I thought they ruined the golf course by redoing it," he said. "I don't know why people don't leave good golf courses alone. The old Oak Hill in '68 was flawless."

Again, what Inman and Trevino weren't taking into account is that many of Ross's courses had become antiquated by mid-1970s standards, and Oak Hill had fallen into that category.

*Chapter 12*

# Golden Bear on the Prowl

Sometime after Jack Nicklaus rolled in his final putt of the third round of the 1980 PGA Championship, the one that finished off a four-under-par 66 that allowed him to take a cozy three-stroke lead into the final eighteen holes, PGA Tour veteran Ed Sneed was heard to remark, "Who does he think he is—Jack Nicklaus again?"

Sneed said it in jest, but everyone in the field legitimately feared it on that August day. Having gone all of 1979 without a victory on the PGA Tour, the first winless season of his fabulous career, there were whispers that perhaps the Golden Bear was finally going into hibernation. The greatest player of his generation (and some would argue of any generation) had hit the wall, and it appeared that he was no longer a true threat to win regular tournaments, let alone major championships.

Yeah, right.

"Everybody has doubts," Nicklaus said recalling that period. "But that didn't eliminate my feeling that I could come back." No. What it did was re-focus the man who had already won sixty-six Tour events, including fifteen majors, four more than runner-up and Rochester native Walter Hagen. True, Nicklaus's everlasting legacy was secure, his fortune was massive and his duty as the sport's ambassador—a torch passed on to him, albeit begrudgingly, by Arnold Palmer—had long been fulfilled. What more did he have to prove?

Well, for starters, he wanted to prove that he could still win. He was in the prime of his life, forty years old as of January 21, 1980. His competitive juices were still flowing, and he knew his game was sharp

Jack Nicklaus had little competition during the 1980 PGA Championship, as he won by a whopping seven strokes.

enough to further his legend. The shot-making ability, the desire, the mental acumen—it was all still there—and he knew there were victories to be won, Tom Watson be damned. It wasn't time to walk away; it was time to become "Jack Nicklaus again."

In his book *My Story*, Nicklaus wrote of his practice regiment before the start of the 1980 season. "All in all, it was the hardest I had worked at golf since my teen years, but the big question remained, would it pay off?" His answer came in June at Baltusrol when he set the U.S. Open scoring record with a 272 total, and when he raised his arms in triumph that Father's Day, the giant scoreboard at the eighteenth green proclaimed, "Jack is Back."

Like he ever really left.

"Why did anyone start saying he was over the hill?" one pro said. "It only made him mad."

So when he arrived at Oak Hill, Nicklaus was—no pun intended—loaded for Bear. And for four days, he stalked the East Course, devouring it as no one ever had, fashioning a seventy-two-hole score of six-under-par 274, still the lowest in Oak Hill's major championship history. It was a magnificent week indeed, and Nicklaus etching his name into Oak Hill lore was only one of several significant moments.

Rochester's own Terry Diehl was a member of the PGA Tour when he competed in the 1980 PGA Championship at his home course.

Before Nicklaus hoisted the Wanamaker Trophy over his head, much of the spotlight shone on Oak Hill's own Craig Harmon, who had been awarded a spot in the field because he was the host PGA professional. A huge gallery filled with members awash with pride followed Harmon during the first two rounds, and even though, as Harmon said, "I shot a million," it was the thrill of a lifetime. "I shot an 89 in the first round, which is far and away the worst score I've ever had in my life," Harmon recalled. And I remember on the first hole…I actually started crying when they announced my name."

On the first hole, barely able to breathe or swing, Harmon hit a terrible drive and an equally poor approach. And as he stood over his chip shot, he remembered thinking, "Please, God, let me at least make contact with this chip shot." He made contact. He also made birdie, as his chip disappeared into the cup and a huge roar shook the canopies of the trees. "I've never had a cheer like that in my life," he said. "I'm one-under on the PGA Tour. I started crying again for getting my ball in the cup. So to say I was an emotional wreck would be an understatement—and I parlayed that birdie into twenty-over-par the next seventeen holes for my 89."

After Harmon missed the cut and returned to the pro shop to sell merchandise, Rochester's own Terry Diehl took his turn on center stage. Diehl was Rochester born and bred and as a teenager had won the Rochester district championship and the New York State Amateur before enjoying a fine career at the University of Georgia. He turned pro and earned his PGA Tour card in the early 1970s, won the 1974 San Antonio Texas Open with a nineteen-under score of 269 and had more than twenty other top-ten finishes, including a tie for seventh in the 1977 U.S. Open. But nothing—not even his victory in San Antonio—could match the excitement he felt playing in his hometown. "I was as nervous as I've ever been," Diehl recalled. "It ranks right up there with my greatest moments. For an athlete to be able to perform in his hometown in front of his friends and family and people who have a rooting interest in him, that was terrific. I was proud to represent Oak Hill and perform at home."

And Oak Hill and Rochester were proud of him. Diehl opened the tournament with a pair of 72s and then carded a splendid third-round 68, which vaulted him into contention, if not for the championship then definitely for a top-eight finish, which would have paid off in an exemption to the 1981 Masters and U.S. Open.

Diehl began the fourth round confident that he could make a move and put some heat on Nicklaus. "I thought I was going to contend; there wasn't any doubt in my mind," he said. A birdie at hole three had his spirits soaring, but in a matter of moments, it all exploded for Diehl. He hit his tee shot on the par-five fourth into the bunker along the right side of the fairway and then watched in horror as his attempt to escape caught the lip of the trap, caromed dead right, bounced off a spectator and came to rest about two inches out of bounds. "Curtis Strange told me it was the worst break he'd ever seen," said Diehl, who went on to make a disastrous triple-bogey from which he never recovered. "For ten years, I never got into a fairway bunker without thinking of that shot. I probably hit a thousand fairway bunker shots in my career, and I always thought

I was pretty good at it. My family was crushed at the end. Everyone was very upset, but what are you going to do?"

Diehl finished with a 76, which dropped him into a tie for tenth and caused him to miss that Masters and U.S. Open exemption by two shots. He then watched Nicklaus do what Nicklaus always seemed to do: close out yet another victory.

Despite his record-setting score in the U.S. Open, Nicklaus wasn't sure what to expect at Oak Hill. He had floundered in recent weeks, a balky putter holding him back, and no one has ever won a major championship with one of those. However, a week before the tournament began, Nicklaus's son Jackie Jr. noticed a technical glitch in his putting stroke, and after working through the problem in the practice rounds, Nicklaus started making everything he looked at.

It was a good thing, too. "I had played fairly well that year," Nicklaus said. "Unfortunately, going into that tournament, I started hitting the ball poorly. And frankly, I hit the ball poorly all week. But my putter was fantastic. I ran the tables with my putter, and it was just a fantastic week."

In his last practice round, Nicklaus meandered around the East Course in sixty-five strokes, needing just one on the new par-three fifteenth, where he holed out with a 4-iron.

When they started keeping score for real, the members must have been wondering why so many players were making a fuss over the course changes, because nine of them broke par in the first round, led by Craig Stadler's 67, a round that he called "fun." That wasn't what he called his second round, though, as he slipped to 75, dropping him four shots behind the new leader, Dr. Gil Morgan. Morgan followed his opening 68 with a 70 and held a one-shot advantage over Nicklaus (70-69) and Lon Hinkle (70-69).

To this point, Nicklaus had played as if he were pacing himself, and it took some work, as he made several par-saving putts to offset errant tee shots or approaches. And then, in the third round, on what is traditionally known as moving day on the tour, Nicklaus made the biggest move of all. Over the first fourteen holes on Saturday, Nicklaus was nearly flawless, and he grabbed firm control of the tournament. He made seven birdies against one bogey, and as he walked to the fifteenth tee, he was seven shots ahead of his nearest pursuer, Hinkle. An uncharacteristic spasm over the last four holes in which he made two bogeys while Hinkle was making a pair of birdies cut his margin to three strokes. He quipped, "After the first fourteen holes, I was ready to come in, but they made me play the last four." Still, his 66 announced to the field that someone was going to have to play a magnificent final round if they were going to overtake him. "The only thing that can catch Nicklaus is the golf course," said John Mahaffey.

The golf course couldn't do it, and neither could Hinkle, Morgan or eventual runner-up Andy Bean. Nicklaus didn't tear it up on Sunday, but he methodically worked his way around and gradually pulled away from the pretenders. He parred every hole on the front nine and stretched his lead to five, and when he birdied holes eleven and thirteen, the only thing left to decide was whether he could break the all-time PGA Championship scoring record of 271. Alas, when he played the final five holes in one-over, he had to be content with the PGA record for margin of victory (seven shots), the Oak Hill seventy-two-hole scoring mark and with tying Hagen's record of five PGA titles.

"I played as fine a finishing round in a major as I've ever played," Nicklaus said of his 69. "Maybe it wasn't too exciting for a lot of people out there, but I had all the excitement I wanted. Oak Hill is a marvelous golf course, and people should not look back at this tournament and look at my score; they should look at how the field did (the average eighteen-hole score was 74.6; Nicklaus's was 68.5). The course is one of the top ten or twelve true championship courses."

*Chapter 13*

# THE KING IS DETHRONED

Jack Nicklaus hadn't even finished off his record-setting romp in the 1980 PGA when, in a meeting room inside Oak Hill's stately clubhouse, club members Allen Brewer, Jerry Stahl and Jack Hoff sat down to talk to PGA of America officials Frank Cardi, Mark Kizzar and Joe Black.

The discussion centered on the 1985 PGA Championship. Having seen what a superb and efficient job Oak Hill had done in hosting the '80 PGA, the organization was prepared, right then and there, to award its '85 Championship to Oak Hill. "I told Frank I needed it in writing," said Brewer, who at that time was the club president. "In September, we got the official offer."

But a funny thing happened on the way to the tournament returning to the East Course. The Oak Hill board, its collective chest puffed out, opted instead to make a run at another U.S. Open. "There is a tendency to feel that the Open is the tournament," said Stahl. "When you see interviews with the players, they usually say the Masters and the Open [are the biggest tournaments]."

The Open hadn't come to Oak Hill since 1968, and after having its advances to host one in the late 1970s declined by the USGA, Oak Hill's movers and shakers believed it was time to ask again. The course had been modernized, and it had certainly flexed its muscles, as the only player in the field to finish under par over seventy-two holes in the '80 PGA was that guy named Nicklaus. The membership had also proven to be masterful in its ability to run a major championship. Oak Hill's Q-rating had never been higher, and the time to strike was now. "It truly was the desire of the club to have a USGA event and to host another Open," said Stahl. "We'd had two U.S. Opens prior to that time, but somehow we lost a little contact with the USGA, so a few of us made a commitment to try and get closer to the USGA and ask what would it take to bring [the Open] back to Oak Hill."

One of the great influences on Miller Barber was Claude Harmon, father of Oak Hill head pro Craig Harmon.

The answer was simple—and quite favorable. The USGA had debuted the U.S. Senior Open at Winged Foot in 1980, but in its first few years of existence, the tournament had lost money, and it was in need of a shot in the arm. "They were trying to promote the Senior Open," said Stahl. "There was no Senior Tour at that time, so they expressed an interest in maybe having Oak Hill hosting the Senior Open as early as we could, and the first year happened to be '84. And that was kind of the steppingstone to get us the U.S. Open in 1989. It brought the USGA back to Oak Hill."

In effect, the Senior Open was a trial balloon. "That was our proving ground as far as the USGA was concerned," said Brewer. "They wanted to see how we would do."

To no one's surprise, Oak Hill did just fine. For the first time in its brief history, the Senior Open netted a profit for the USGA, thanks to Oak Hill's expert organizational work and the support from the community, which turned out in record numbers to watch Miller Barber outduel the great Arnold Palmer down the stretch. Barely seven months later, in February 1985, then–USGA president Jim Hand, clearly impressed with Oak Hill, asked the club if it would like to host the 1989 U.S. Open. A few months before the '89 Open was played, Hand said:

Arnold Palmer watches his tee shot at the fifth hole.

> *I had it in my mind, all things being equal, that I would try and promote them. I saw the organization and the buildup to the Senior Open for two years, and you could see it was going to be successful. The basic criteria* [for selecting U.S. Open sites] *is the quality of the golf course. It's a great golf course—you take that for granted. The rest of it is all the other facilities they have and the people who are involved. Oak Hill has a great clubhouse, a sizable membership and is in a great community that supports golf.*

The biggest name in the field, of course, was Palmer, and the King put on quite a show. But it wasn't quite good enough to snatch the victory from the man who was nicknamed the Mysterious Mr. X. Barber stared down one of the game's all-time greats, on one of the game's all-time difficult courses, and whipped them both on the strength of a classic display of clutch final-round shot making. "It was very exciting that day," Barber recalled of his final-round 71, which was just good enough to outlast Palmer by two strokes. "I had played a lot of golf with Arnold, and we were very good friends. That day I just thought, 'I'm playing with the King, and if I could beat him, that would be very, very special.'"

This particular tournament is remembered largely for the one-inch putt that Palmer missed at the fifteenth hole on Sunday that resulted in a painful double-bogey. However, Palmer was already two strokes behind at the time, so it wasn't like that ignominious gaffe cost him the tournament. Make no mistake; Palmer did not lose—Barber won.

Winning was something that Barber wasn't capable of when he first broke out on the regular tour in 1959. In fact, had it not been for a hole-in-one he made during the 1961 Seattle Open, which paid him $10,000, he would have been unable to pay off his sponsors and may very well have left the tour. "In the early '60s, when I started out, I played for a couple years, and I didn't do that much," he recalled. "A lot of great players told me, 'You need to go up [to New York] and work and refine your game.' They told me, 'You can play out here, but you need to learn a few things.'"

At that time, many of the game's great teachers were working in the Metropolitan PGA section, not the least of whom was Oak Hill pro Craig Harmon's father, Claude Harmon, who was at Winged Foot. Barber took a job as an assistant pro at the Apawamis Club in Rye under the guidance of head pro Jacques Patroni, and while he was in New York, he would visit teachers such as Harmon and Herman Barron, seeking swing tips and wisdom. Barber recalled:

> *I'd call them up to ask for help, and they'd help me. Claude Harmon taught me how to play out of the sand. He was one of the best who ever lived, and he'd say, "Come on over to Winged Foot and I'll show you some shots." Then he'd go out and hit some balls, show me some odds and ends, tell me what my strong points were and what my weak points were. He was a great man—very dedicated to the game. He taught me not only how to play out of the sand but how to be a gentleman—to say "Yes sir" and "No sir." He'd say, "You'd be surprised how that will have an effect on people," and he was right. It was growing up for me. I was just a country boy from Texas who didn't have the experience of dealing with people.*

Barber won eleven events during a twenty-year career on the regular tour, the last coming in 1978, when he won the Phoenix Open at the age of forty-six. He joined the Senior Tour in 1981 and after failing to win a regular major won a Senior major four years in a row from 1982 to 1985 (three U.S. Senior Opens in 1982, '84 and '85, and the Senior Players Championship in '83).

Barber finished tied for twenty-fourth with a ten-over total of 290 in the 1968 Open at Oak Hill, but he was convinced he would do much better his second time around in 1984. "I had played the course, knew what a great golf course it was and I remembered some of the foul-ups I had made in '68, so I just thought, 'Don't come back and make the same old mistakes,'" said Barber.

Bob Goalby set the early pace, as he was the only player to match par-70 on the first day. "It's the longest darn 6,700-yard golf course I've ever seen," said Goalby. "I've never seen the pin placements this tough in a national championship," said Billy Casper, who shot a 77 and called the course conditions "impossible."

Barber got around in 74, matching Palmer's score, but he couldn't keep pace with Arnie on the second day, as Palmer surged in front with an electrifying 68. Palmer played the front side in two-over, but he birdied holes twelve, thirteen, sixteen and seventeen for a back-side 31, putting him two shots ahead of Goalby and three clear of Barber, who shot 71.

Palmer maintained a one-stroke lead over Barber with a third-round 72, even though, in his words, he "didn't make a putt all day." Meanwhile, Barber crafted a 70 to work his way into the final twosome with Palmer. And although Barber knew Palmer was going to be the people's choice, he cracked, "He'll have his five thousand [fans], and I'll have my three or four." But Barber wasn't backing down at all from the challenge of playing—and beating—Palmer.

The action was fast and furious at the start of the fourth round. Palmer bogeyed the second hole but came right back to regain the lead with a birdie at number three. Barber fell two shots back when he bogeyed number four, but the turning point in the round occurred at the fifth hole. Palmer drove into the fairway bunker, splashed his approach into Allen's Creek and wound up with a bogey, while Barber stuck a pitching wedge to three feet and converted for birdie, a two-shot swing that created a tie atop the leaderboard.

From there, Palmer bogeyed holes seven, ten and eleven, while Barber embarked on a string of ten consecutive pars, putting him three shots ahead. Barber knew Arnie would make a charge, and it looked like it was coming when he made a birdie on fourteen. However, the charge came to an abrupt and stunning halt at the par-three fifteenth. Palmer and his caddie, Creamy Carolan, disagreed on club selection. Palmer wanted to hit an 8-iron, while Carolan suggested a 7-iron. Palmer deferred to Carolan and hit the 7-iron over the back edge of the green. "The yardage said 7-iron, but I wanted to hit the 8," Palmer said. "Creamy talked me out of it." Palmer was visibly aggravated, and the situation intensified

Arnold Palmer and his caddie, Creamy Carolan, discuss their options on the fifteenth tee during the final round.

a few minutes later when Carolan swore at spectators on the way to the green and Palmer chewed him out.

Palmer chipped ten feet past the hole, missed his par-saver by an inch and, when he went to tap that in, stubbed his putter and never touched the ball. No one in the world knew he'd done it, but Palmer called the stroke on himself, and before Barber attempted his three-footer for par, Arnie said, "I made five."

Barber was so shocked that he missed his putt and made bogey, yet he still increased his lead back to three strokes thanks to Palmer's double-bogey. "I didn't see him miss that putt," Barber recalled. "I couldn't believe it. In my wildest imagination, I wouldn't have known he had done it if he hadn't spoken up."

Palmer didn't quit. He made birdie at sixteen, and when Barber pushed his drive into trouble at seventeen, the door was open for a miracle Palmer rally. Instead, Barber rifled a 2-iron into the fairway just short of the green. "It was one of the best shots of my life," he said. He then wedged to three feet to save par. With a two-stroke cushion, he calmly ripped a drive down the middle at eighteen, hit a 6-iron to three feet and cautiously two-putted for his winning par.

At the closing ceremony, despite the bitter taste of defeat still on his palate, Palmer told the gathered throng, "Oak Hill and this town have given the USGA something to hang its hat on. The Senior Open here was the most successful we've ever had. I only hope they [the USGA] remember that when the time comes."

Palmer was referring to Oak Hill's desire to host an Open, for which a decision by the USGA was on the horizon. USGA president James Hand laughed and responded, "Don't worry, we'll remember."

*Chapter 14*

# Move Over, Ben

Six years hence, Curtis Strange sat on a makeshift stage set up along the ninth hole of Oak Hill's West Course, his head buried in his hands and overcome with emotion after a long, grueling and bitterly disappointing weekend during which he played a central role in the United States losing the Ryder Cup matches in 1995.

Those three September days were in stark contrast to Strange's previous visit to Rochester in June 1989, a glorious four-day sojourn that concluded with him sitting in the press room moments after becoming the first man since Ben Hogan in 1951 to win back-to-back U.S. Open championships and smiling broadly as he uttered the words, "Move over, Ben."

Of all the greats who have competed at Oak Hill, there is no player who has a more dichotomous history with the club than Strange. "It was feast or famine for me there," Strange said with a smile a few years ago.

But here's the thing. While many athletes will tell you that they usually remember the pain of the defeats far more than they remember the joy of the triumphs, Strange won't allow himself to do so. Winning the U.S. Open, the tournament he considers the most important in all of golf, usurps what happened in the Ryder Cup when he lost all three of the matches he played in, including the critical singles match against Nick Faldo that pretty much sealed America's fate. "It doesn't color the way I remember the course; it actually maybe enhances it a bit," he said of the Ryder Cup disappointment. "Oak Hill means a great deal to me because it represents one of the best moments in my life and one of the toughest moments in my life. If you play

Curtis Strange became the first man since Ben Hogan in 1950 and 1951 to win back-to-back U.S. Open titles.

golf long enough, you're going to have tough times, and they are not to be forgotten. But Oak Hill doesn't diminish at all because of not playing well in the Ryder Cup."

In reality, when Strange came to Oak Hill in 1995 as a somewhat controversial captain's pick of his good friend Lanny Wadkins, it was going to be next to impossible for him to top the excitement and achievement of winning the Open in '89, and he knew that. "I don't care what they say about other golf tournaments, but your Open championship is your Open championship," Strange said. "The Ryder Cup is a team event, and I didn't play well. But there were a number of others who didn't as well. I take partial blame, but I don't take all of it. You put it in perspective, and it was an exciting week. But once again, it's an event versus your Open championship. There's a big difference."

Oak Hill had hosted five major tournaments to this point, but none of them generated the buzz of the 1989 Open. After a twenty-one-year absence, the Open was back, and Rochester was electric as the days wound down to that moment on Thursday morning when balls permeated the air. The tickets were all sold out, corporate hospitality sales had set Open records, the course was manicured to perfection and the club was more than ready to have the eyes of the world upon it. And if that wasn't enough to tantalize the senses, there was the much-anticipated return of favorite son Jeff Sluman, the Greece native and Oak Hill honorary member who had won the 1988 PGA Championship, securing his chance to compete in his hometown for the first time as a member of the PGA Tour.

However, some of the excitement regarding Sluman's appearance was quelled, thanks to an unfortunate and terribly timed complication. A month before the Open was to be played, Sluman fell ill while playing in Jack Nicklaus's Memorial Tournament outside Columbus, Ohio. On the morning of the final round, he rushed himself to a hospital and underwent an emergency appendectomy. His surgery was successful. He followed doctors' orders and didn't touch a golf club for a couple weeks, but that's no way to get prepared to play in a U.S. Open.

Sluman was determined to play at Oak Hill, and he started practicing seventeen days after the operation. And though he reported no pain—except when he unleashed a couple of drivers—it was obvious that the surgery would hinder him. He felt he was well enough to test himself in competition the week before the Open at the Westchester Classic, and he performed well, all things considered. On a tough course similar in style to Oak Hill, he shot 72-69-70-75 and finished tied for thirty-second, nine shots behind winner Wayne Grady.

But in the difficult major championship conditions of the East Course, not even Sluman's home-course advantage was enough to overcome his less-than-100-percent physical stature. Playing in a dream threesome with legends and past Oak Hill major championship winners Nicklaus and Lee

Trevino in front of thousands of spectators who followed only that group, he shot rounds of 75-71, missing the cut by one skinny stroke. "He actually played pretty good," said Craig Harmon, Oak Hill's head pro and Sluman's longtime coach. "He was very, very tired. I mean, he could hardly walk around the golf course, but his adrenaline was going, and stuff kept him

Greece native Jeff Sluman missed the cut in his first major championship at Oak Hill, partly because he was just coming off emergency appendectomy surgery.

going. He had this great pairing for two rounds, and he just wasn't physically fit to compete. I was really more disappointed for him knowing that he was not going to be 100 percent—if he could play at all—and how much it meant to him."

Sluman took it in stride and said:

> *I can look myself in the eye and say I did the best I could. But considering what happened to me health-wise, I think I'm fortunate just to have been able to play. It was disappointing in the aspect that I wasn't physically capable of playing the golf I thought I could, but that's just the way it goes. It's not really a hiccup or a big deal in my life. You miss it by one, and everyone says, "Is there one shot you remember?" Well, if you start thinking like that, you'll drive yourself crazy.*

Speaking of driving yourself crazy, that's how Strange was feeling after he tied the East Course record of six-under-par 64, originally set by Hogan, the man whose legend he was chasing that week. There is inherent pressure for every competitor who embarks on his defense of a major championship, and Strange had certainly felt that in the year since his breakthrough triumph in 1988 at Brookline Country Club in Massachusetts. "It was exciting, hectic and stressful—but also something you wouldn't trade for the world," Strange said. "It was what you strive to do."

Strange grew up in Virginia, the son of a golf professional, and when he was twelve years old he made the decision to give up playing all of the other sports that he loved in order to concentrate on golf. "I was just like any other kid," said Strange. "I would go to the course [White Sands Country Club in Virginia Beach, which was owned by his father, Tom] and start playing, and I fell in love with the game and the whole country club atmosphere. But when I went to the course, I didn't practice for twelve hours a day like people might think. I got in trouble and messed around just like any other kid."

Still, Strange became proficient enough to attend Wake Forest University—alma mater of his hero, Arnold Palmer—and after some early success there, he knew he was going to pursue a career on the PGA Tour. He left Wake Forest after his junior year, failed in his first attempt to gain his Tour card in the fall of 1976 but survived Qualifying School in the spring of 1977. He won only three times in his first six years, but starting in 1983, he won at least one tournament for seven consecutive seasons, a total of fourteen wins during that stretch. He peaked in 1988 when he became the

Nick Price, Jerry Pate, Mark Wiebe and Doug Weaver all made holes-in-one at the sixth hole within a span of two hours during the second round of the 1989 U.S. Open.

first player to earn $1 million in one season, and one of his four victories came in the U.S. Open when he defeated Faldo in an eighteen-hole playoff.

In the first half of 1989, Strange had six top-ten finishes in fifteen starts when he teed it up for the first round at Oak Hill, and by the end of that day, after a solid but unspectacular one-over 71, he sat five shots behind co-leaders Payne Stewart, Bernhard Langer and Jay Don Blake, who matched scorching 66s. In fact, Strange was not one of the record twenty-one players who broke par, but one of those who was, Tom Kite, eerily remarked, "When all is said and done, Oak Hill will get its licks in." Oh, did that statement eventually ring true for Kite.

And while Kite was proven correct, that didn't happen in the second round, a historic day on which Strange shot his 64 to vault into the lead by one over Kite. And four players—Doug Weaver, Mark Wiebe, Jerry Pate and Nick Price—all made holes-in-one at the 167-yard sixth hole within a two-hour span in the morning. Fred Funk, who came through shortly after the last ace and made a birdie, turned to the gallery and said, "I can't believe you're clapping for a two."

The clapping that could be heard on day three was for greens superintendent Joe Hahn and his army of staffers, as they performed a minor miracle in getting the course in shape for play after torrential rain poured from the heavens overnight. "I guess the biggest thing that happened that week was the rain we had Friday night," said Jerry Stahl, who served as co-chairman of the tournament along with Allen Brewer. "I woke up Saturday morning and was coming out to the club. I think it was the crack of dawn, five-thirty or so, and I was half asleep driving down Chapin Way, and the first thing I saw was a lake on the eighth fairway. I can remember saying to myself, 'I don't remember a lake being on the eighth fairway.'"

Hahn and his crew were at work shortly thereafter, and their Herculean efforts enabled play to begin in the early afternoon. And somehow, the round was completed just as dusk was turning to darkness. "I think it's a tribute to the type of people we had working here and the type of superintendents working around this community and their willingness to come over and help us pull it off," Hahn said. "I've seen Opens where they've had one or two bunkers washed out. I'm talking about thirty, forty bunkers that were washed out that morning. We had 1.9 inches of rain between ten o'clock when we left there [Friday] night and five in the morning when we got back."

During the mushy, rain-delayed third round, Strange struggled to a 73, and when the long day was over, Kite's second straight 69 sent him into the lead with eighteen holes to go, one ahead of Scott Simpson and three clear of Strange. "A lot of people who entered the tournament would love to have the chance to be scared to death," Kite said of the impending final round.

Tom Kite seemed to be cruising to his first major championship until a disastrous triple-bogey at the fifth hole on Sunday.

It would not be a stretch to say that no one would have loved to go through the trauma that Kite inflicted on himself during his gruesome final round, which saw him flame out with a 78, killing his chances of winning his first major championship. He seemed to be in command when he managed pars on the first two holes, birdied number three and parred number four. He'd stretched his lead on Simpson to three shots and to four over Strange by the time he'd stepped onto the tee at the par-four fifth. But during the next twenty minutes, it all came unraveled.

Kite pushed his drive into Allen's Creek, missed the green with his third shot and then three-putted from twelve feet for a triple-bogey that sent shock waves around the East Course. Strange heard about Kite's gaffe while playing the eighth hole, and he remembered thinking, "When Tom made the triple bogey, I felt like it played right into my hands." That's because Strange was methodically moving his way around the East Course in even par, and while Kite allowed a number of players back into the tournament (seven were within one shot of the lead at one point), it was now Strange's tournament to win, and everyone knew it. "My whole strategy was that, if you just hang long enough in an Open, which Nicklaus did many, many times, you don't have to make many birdies," Strange said. "If you hang in there and play solid golf, you can sometimes be the last guy standing—you can survive. And that is what an Open test is: survival."

Kite went on to bogey holes eight and ten, handing Strange the lead for good, and added double-bogeys at thirteen and fifteen to cap his horrible day. Japan's Jumbo Ozaki drew even with Strange when he birdied number ten, but bogeys on fourteen, sixteen and eighteen eliminated him.

Mark McCumber made a birdie at sixteen to get close, but he couldn't beat par on seventeen and eighteen. Ian Woosnam's birdies at fifteen and eighteen were too little, too late, while Chip Beck parred the last six holes, which only enabled him to tread water. So Strange continued on his merry way, aggravated that he couldn't make a birdie but perfectly aware that par was good enough.

Strange was in trouble at fifteen when he missed the green and left his chip seven feet short, but he knocked in that pressure-packed putt to remain in front. He then lasered a 6-iron approach at sixteen to ten feet and rolled in the birdie. "The birdie at sixteen was so important," he said. "If there was a shot that won the tournament for me, that was it. And when my drive hit the fairway at seventeen and my 3-iron hit the green, I was feeling pretty good."

After an easy par at seventeen, Strange hit another perfect drive at eighteen, and when his 6-iron landed safely on the green, he climbed the steep embankment that led to the putting surface and thrust his fist into the air, much to the delight of the overflow gallery. Even though he three-putted for bogey, he knew no one left on the course was likely to catch him, and his score of two-under 278 was one stroke clear of already-finished runners-up Beck, McCumber and Woosnam.

"It's not so much what Hogan did," Strange said, referring to his successful defense of the Open crown, a feat that has not been duplicated since, "it's what others have not done. The great Arnold Palmer, Jack Nicklaus and Tom Watson have not won back-to-back Opens." Neither did the likes of Walter Hagen, Byron Nelson, Gene Sarazen, Gary Player, Lee Trevino, Johnny Miller or, as of yet, Tiger Woods, Phil Mickelson or Rory McIlroy. "You play your whole life to throw up on yourself on Sunday afternoon at the Open," Strange said. "It was absolutely the pinnacle for me." And that's because strangely enough, even though he was in the prime of his career, Strange never won another PGA Tour event. He recalled:

> *It wasn't like I didn't put the effort in because I won the Open twice and just said, "Screw it, I don't have to do anything else." I put in plenty of effort—I just didn't play well. And every effort physically is one thing, but being into it mentally is something else, and I don't think I ever quite got into it mentally again. You've got to take the bad with the good, because the game is going to do it to you. Many of mine* [the good and bad] *happened to be on a big stage, but I would rather do that than not be on the stage at all.*

*Chapter 15*

# Greatness in the Golf Shop

Craig Harmon's fellow PGA Club Professional Hall of Famer Jim Mrva, who works a few miles away from Oak Hill at another Donald Ross–designed course, Monroe Golf Club, calls Harmon "the best club pro in the country."

Craig's famous golf instructor brother, Butch, who has mentored the likes of Tiger Woods and Phil Mickelson among many other superstar PGA Tour pros, gets all the headlines and golf magazine spreads, but he also defers to Craig as the best in the business. And you're not going to get an argument from anyone at Oak Hill, as the club is privileged to have had Harmon running its golf operation for forty-one years now. "What he brings to the table is that he's the consummate pro," said Oak Hill member Bill Westerfeld, who joined the club in 1973, just a few months after Harmon had been hired. "First and foremost, he's a terrific human being. He's certainly one of the best teaching pros in the world, and he has an enormous love for helping players of all levels reach their potential. He gets a big kick out of teaching. You'd have to spend twelve hours in the sun watching us hackers go out there and slap at the ball. That's one of his greatest assets."

In the fall of 1972, head pro Jack Lumpkin caught Oak Hill off guard by resigning the position. The golf committee quickly tabbed Bill Thaney Sr., who has been a member at Oak Hill since 1946, and the late Joe King to head the search committee to find a replacement.

More than fifty applicants were reviewed, and a select group of men were interviewed, including Mickey Powell, who later became president of the PGA, and Hubie Smith, who had just been named PGA Club Professional of the Year. But when the exhaustive process was complete, one man stood above the others. This young unknown was named Craig Harmon, and his greatest attribute at the time may have been simply that he was the second-oldest of four sons fathered by 1948 Masters champion and legendary Winged Foot head pro Claude Harmon. "Craig was only twenty-six years old, had limited experience, had never been a head pro, was not a PGA member, looked like he was seventeen and had an Army Reserve obligation that would take him away for two weeks each summer—and there were probably a couple of other negatives also," said Bill Reeves, who was on that search committee and has been a member at Oak Hill since 1949.

However, the club could not ignore Harmon's pedigree, nor could the committee find anyone who left a better impression than Harmon. Reeves said of Craig:

> *I will never forget the day he came for his interview. He blew away the competition. I think it was on this day that Thaney asked him whether he would leave Oak Hill to take the Winged Foot job if it became available, and Craig said, "I will make Oak Hill my Winged Foot." Looking back on it, one would have to say that hiring Craig was a very gutsy call by the committee and the board. He has made us all look good.*

"I think he is as good a representative of Oak Hill or any club as anyone would want," Thaney said. "He has no peers around the country. To have him [speaking] up there on the podium…I don't know if any pro handles himself as well as he does."

To this day, Harmon can still recall the excitement he felt when he learned that he was the choice, and he still counts it as the grandest achievement of his career. "When Joe King and Bill Thaney called me and told me I would be the head pro at Oak Hill, you can't top that," he said. "Everything that has happened in my life is because those two men took a chance on me. I've been lucky to have a lot of things happen, but it all happened when they decided to take a gamble on me."

During his long and distinguished career, Harmon has reached the highest plateaus in his profession. In 2000, he was named one of the top fifty teachers in the world; he was selected as the PGA Club Professional of the Year in 2004; and he was inducted into the PGA Club Pro Hall of Fame in 2005. Locally, in the Western New York PGA section, he has been named Teacher of the Year four times (1986, 1991, 1995, 2002), was the 1983 Golf Professional of the Year, the 1993 section Horton Smith Award (education)

Craig Harmon spends time working with his prized pupil, Greece's Jeff Sluman.

winner and is enshrined in the Hall of Fame. At Oak Hill, he was afforded the club's highest honor when he was inducted into the Hill of Fame in 2003.

Like his predecessors, Lumpkin and Charlie McKenna, Harmon was a terrific player, but his own game has always taken a back seat to the needs of the club and its members. "He's always got a game plan," said Westerfeld. "He's always looking for ways to improve things, and he wants to help the membership enjoy the game more. That's good business."

"Teaching is the most rewarding thing we can do in our business," said Harmon, who has been Rochester native Jeff Sluman's swing coach for more than thirty years. "We actually get a chance to help someone with their game, and their smile is our tremendous award. The modern professional should make teaching their top priority."

Through the years, Harmon has had opportunities to take his considerable talents elsewhere. But it has always been his belief that he could never be in a better situation or a better place than he is in at Oak Hill. "It has nothing to do with money; it has everything to do with people," said Harmon, who has four children with his wife, Sandy, all of whom were born in Rochester. "The marriage I've had with the members of Oak Hill can't be replaced anywhere in the country."

Jack Lumpkin spent nearly ten years as Oak Hill's head pro and was credited with teaching the club how to merchandise.

"He is a total gentleman, an outstanding teacher, a mentor to countless youngsters who have revered him and who learned from him much more than their golf swings and the best pro we have ever had," said Reeves.

Lumpkin's ten-year tenure from 1963 to 1972 at Oak Hill was quite short, especially in comparison to the forty-one years Harmon has worked at the club and the thirty-five years McKenna served as the head pro from 1926 to 1960. However, Lumpkin did great work and set a solid foundation for Harmon to build on, because in the early to mid-1960s, the game of golf was beginning to change, and Lumpkin was well ahead of the curve. No longer was it the golf pro's job to just play with the members and give lessons, which was McKenna's forte. Golf had become an industry, and that meant turning a profit in the pro shop. And Lumpkin showed Oak Hill how to do that. "Jack and his wife, Sherry, were magnificent merchandisers," said Thaney. "He showed us a complete new era as to what the golf professional was all about. I think that was a great step. It was the first time we were showing off our logo."

Lumpkin sold merchandise adorned with the classic acorn logo, but his contributions to the flourishing of Oak Hill did not stop there. Taking a cue from his mentor, Claude Harmon, Lumpkin knew how to train assistant pros, as five men who worked under him at Oak Hill went on to head professional jobs. "Claude Harmon said that he always looked for gentlemen with good character and that with that foundation plus good training, he could always make a good professional," Lumpkin said. "I always thought that was a great philosophy."

Lumpkin, who played on the PGA Tour in the 1950s and competed in three U.S. Opens and a PGA Championship, worked under Claude Harmon at Winged Foot before taking the head pro job at Echo Lake in New Jersey. Oak Hill hired him on the recommendation of Harmon. He played a key role in establishing Oak Hill's junior golf program and accompanied three of his pupils—Chuck Ryan, Bobby Hoff and Doug Miller—to the 1969 National Junior Championship.

As a player, Lumpkin set the West Course record with a 66 (it has since been broken) while in the company of members Howie Anderson, Al Schieble and Bob Pecquinot. "We played the Anderson blues that day—the blue tees and then three paces back," Lumpkin recalled. "Howie said he would play me even that day because he always played pros even from the blue tees. I asked him if he ever beat anybody, and he said, 'I don't beat many, but when I do, we run them out of town.'"

In 1972, Lumpkin asked King, then the club president, to release him from his contract because of an opportunity that had arisen at Sea Island in his native state of Georgia. He went on to excel as a teacher, working on the staff of the Golf Digest Schools for about twenty-five years. The 1995 PGA Teacher of the Year has worked with numerous PGA stars, including Sea Island resident and 2012 Ryder Cup captain Davis Love III.

"Jack was fun…he was a heck of a guy," said Thaney. "He was one of those guys who knew everybody and acknowledged everybody. That was

Oak Hill head professional Craig Harmon (left) was inducted into the Hill of Fame in 2003.

Bill Reeves congratulates LPGA Hall of Famer Betsy Rawls, who was inducted into the Hill of Fame in 2010.

Jack Nicklaus is congratulated by PGA of America president Frank Cardi after winning the 1980 PGA, his seventeenth professional major championship victory.

Curtis Strange climbs the embankment in front of the eighteenth green, moments away from securing his victory in the 1989 U.S. Open.

*Right*: After failing in his first two attempts in 1991 and 1993, European captain Bernard Gallacher was finally able to hold aloft the Ryder Cup in 1995.

*Below*: Tom Lehman celebrates his singles victory over Seve Ballesteros, one of the few bright spots on that fateful Sunday.

*Left*: 1997 U.S. Amateur champ Matt Kuchar saw his defense end when he lost to Sergio Garcia in the quarterfinals of the 1998 Amatuer.

*Below*: Hank Kuehne drove it for miles at Oak Hill, but his putting was just as important as his prodigious tee shots.

*Above*: Tiger Woods's first appearance at Oak Hill in the 2003 PGA resulted in a tie for thirty-ninth place.

*Right*: Shaun Micheel stares at his ball, sitting two inches from the cup on the eighteenth green, before securing his stunning victory in the 2003 PGA.

Phil Mickelson shot a 66 in the first round of the 2003 PGA but followed with a 75 and never contended thereafter.

The huge gallery around the eighteenth hole on Sunday afternoon of the 2003 PGA.

*Above*: Shaun Micheel follows through with his 7-iron approach at eighteen, one of the great shots in PGA Championship history.

*Right*: Shaun Micheel's PGA victory was his first as a member of the Tour

A view of the back of the clubhouse during its most recent renovation.

View of the Hill of Fame and the thirteenth green.

View of the East Course's fifteenth green.

View of the East Course's eighteenth hole.

View of the back of the clubhouse.

Ben Hogan once called the East Course's first hole the toughest starting hole in golf.

The eighth hole is part of a difficult stretch of four consecutive par-fours in the middle of the layout.

Allens Creek looms dangerously to the left and behind the sixth green, where four players made holes-in-one in a two-hour span during the second round of the 1989 U.S. Open.

A look down the tenth hole, where a pinpoint drive to a sloping fairway is a necessity.

Englishman Howard Clark made an ace at the eleventh hole, spurring his singles victory over Peter Jacobsen in the 1995 Ryder Cup.

The short, uphill par-four fourteenth is an exciting tournament hole because the long-hitting players will often try to drive the green.

The well-bunkered seventeenth hole, a par-five for members but a par-four for the professionals, was the site of Jay Haas's third-round hole-out for eagle in the 2008 Senior PGA Championship.

View of the Tudor-style clubhouse from the front, with Chapin Way leading to the front entrance.

View of the eighteenth green from the right rough, with the majestic clubhouse looming in the background.

Charlie McKenna (middle) was Oak Hill's head pro for thirty-five years, retiring in 1960.

part of what we saw in a pro for the first time. Charlie would say hello, but that was about it. Jack really lit up the place."

McKenna's ties to Oak Hill stretched back to World War I. He was a member of Oak Hill when it was still located at its original Genesee River site in downtown Rochester, and he was one of its finest players, as he won the club championship three years in a row (1919–21). He turned pro in 1922 and went to work at Irondequoit Country Club for three years before taking the head job at Oak Hill when the club moved to its Pittsford address in 1926.

As a player, McKenna won scores of local events, and he also won the PGA Seniors Championship in 1948 at PGA National with a three-under-par score of 141. He also played in some of the major events that were held at Oak Hill in the 1940s, such as the 1941 and 1942 Times-Union Opens. When he wasn't perfecting his own game, competing in area tournaments, playing exhibition matches against visiting professionals at Oak Hill or serving as host professional for the 1949 Amateur and the 1956 Open, he was shaping the swings of hundreds of Oak Hill members.

Chip Lillich, one of Oak Hill's most decorated players who also holds the record for most Rochester District Golf Association championships with eight, was ten years old when his grandfather, Jim Weldon, a fine player in his own right, took him to see McKenna for lessons. Lillich recalled of McKenna:

> *He was almost like an uncle to me because my grandfather and he were very close friends. I started under him when I was ten and worked with him until he retired in 1960. He was quite an important person in my development as a golfer. Charlie knew the finer points of the game. You could go out there and hit four balls, and Charlie knew what you were doing wrong. He had a terrific eye—very, very fine. He was a great golfer, too. I had a chance to caddie for him a fair amount because my grandfather played a lot with him, and I learned a lot caddying for him. He was a quiet man. He didn't say too much or have a big, outgoing personality, but he was a fine man. He was honest and trustworthy, and he really liked to see people develop as golfers.*

*Chapter 16*

# HEARTBREAK HILL

Oak Hill member Bob Skipworth was standing next to the tenth tee at Jack Nicklaus's Muirfield Village course on the afternoon of September 26, 1987. And just like every other spectator in the gallery that day, he was captivated by the passion and excitement the twenty-seventh Ryder Cup Matches were producing.

Skipworth, then the vice-president of Oak Hill, was there as a fan and was not representing Oak Hill in any type of official capacity. But with one seemingly innocuous question that he asked of former PGA of America president Joe Black, he may as well have been. "I had just watched Tom Kite, Curtis Strange, Nick Faldo and Ian Woosnam tee off," Skipworth said. "We were standing there, and Joe Black came along and said, 'Oh, there's a few familiar faces.' I asked Joe, 'How does a guy like Jack Nicklaus and Muirfield Village get the Ryder Cup?' And he said, 'Well, he asked for it.'"

Ding, ding, ding. That response turned the inside of Skipworth's head into a pinball machine, and Black, who knew Skipworth and many Oak Hill members from when he was the PGA of America czar in 1980, the year Oak Hill hosted the PGA Championship, was hearing the same buzzers and bells blaring. Skipworth recalled:

> *Joe asked me why I had asked, and then he said, "Do you think you guys at Oak Hill would be interested in the Ryder Cup?" We had the U.S. Open coming in 1989, but we had a long talk about it, and then later on, I saw Joe again and said, "You know, the more I think about it, the more I'd like*

*to go back to our board with that." He said he'd talk to his people, and that was that.*

Exactly four years to the day later, Skipworth and a delegation of Oak Hill members sat down with PGA officials at Kiawah Island, South Carolina, where the 1991 matches were being hotly contested, and signed a contract to host the 1995 Ryder Cup. "I was exhilarated," Skipworth said. "I felt great for the community—for Rochester. It's one of the great tournaments in the world. It was really exciting."

Exciting? Of all the events that have been held at Oak Hill, there has never been anything quite like the 1995 Ryder Cup. Although not among the recognized four major championships, you can make the case (and many golf observers have) that the biennial matches are the most compelling event in golf. And no one who attended the thirty-first renewal of this America-versus-Europe spectacle at Oak Hill would argue that point.

Trailing 9-7 after the first two days of competition, the European team, which was considered a heavy underdog on American soil before the matches began, pulled off what to that point was the greatest come-from-behind victory in Ryder Cup history. The Hill of Fame plaque that honors the 1995 European Ryder Cup team reads: "Their magnificent comeback victory is in the first rank of the most stirring triumphs in the history of golf and reminds us, once again, why golf is the best of games."

Yes, that about sums it up.

The prevailing storyline in the days leading up to the start of the event was: "How can the European team even stay close to this American all-star squad?"

The United States was led by the fiery Corey Pavin, who three months earlier had won the U.S. Open at Shinnecock Hills. There were rising superstars Davis Love III and Phil Mickelson; established veterans such as Fred Couples, Ben Crenshaw, Peter Jacobsen, Jay Haas and Curtis Strange; and up-and-coming players like Loren Roberts, Tom Lehman, Jeff Maggert and Brad Faxon. This was a deep, well-balanced, multitalented team playing a home game.

The Europeans had crusty veterans Nick Faldo, Bernhard Langer and Colin Montgomerie, but from that solid base, the talent pool dipped precipitously. Seve Ballesteros and Ian Woosnam hadn't been playing well in recent years; Mark James, Howard Clark and Sam Torrance were well past their primes; Costantino Rocca had just lost a playoff at the British Open to John Daly, and his confidence was further eroded by his loss to Love in a key singles match in the 1993 Ryder Cup that cemented the U.S. victory at the Belfry in England; and the Americans had barely heard of youngsters Per-Ulrik Johansson, David Gilford and Philip Walton.

Fred Couples produced a match record of 2-1-1, but it wasn't enough to deliver a victory for the United States.

No wonder the British press—as well as most of the American press—were predicting a United States wipeout. But European captain Bernard Gallacher and his team merely shrugged their shoulders, paying no attention to what the voracious tabloids were saying. "It was never going to be the write-off that the British press was forecasting," Gallacher recalled a year after the matches when he returned to Oak Hill to represent his team at its Hill of Fame induction ceremony. "They got it wrong. I felt the matches were always going to be close. Just because it was in America, I didn't think it was going to be that big an advantage. The teams looked pretty evenly balanced to me."

It didn't start well for Europe, though. Playing in weather that should have suited them just fine, the Europeans struggled on the first day, as a cold, steady rain produced miserable conditions. Unfazed by the weather, the partisan crowd roared long and loud throughout, as the Americans captured five of the eight available points. The key development was Europe's top duo of Faldo and Montgomerie losing twice—1-up to Pavin and Lehman in the morning foursomes and 3 and 2 in the afternoon four-ball to Couples and Love.

"Well, with the guys they were playing—Tom Lehman, Corey Pavin, Davis Love and Fred Couples—they aren't any slouches," Wadkins said. "They can beat anyone in the world when they're playing good. Faldo and Montgomerie struggled a little here and there, but they ran into some guys who played some pretty good golf. I'm sure it surprises them, but I thought my guys were going to beat them. Faldo and Montgomerie lost to four pretty damn good players."

Wadkins, despite being chilled to the bone, was feeling pretty good about the day. But he cautioned his team, "This is only day one—no one awards trophies for being the first-round leader. They have a lot of experienced champions, and they aren't going to lie down by any stretch of the imagination."

Over in Europe's team room, there was certainly no panic. "I wasn't thrilled that they were ahead, but two points isn't all that much when you have a lot of matches to play yet," said Langer. "We were in good spirits because over the years, the Americans were always favorites on paper. Even when we won it two or three times in a row, they were still favorites on paper. But paper doesn't hit the balls, and it's a lot about team effort and getting your game in shape for those three days. It just meant we had to play even harder."

Sure enough, Europe came out swinging the next morning, as it won three of the four foursomes matches to even the score at 6-6. Playing in cool but sunny conditions, Europe seemed to hit all the clutch shots and big putts in that session. Rocca, playing with Woosnam, made a hole-in-one at six that kick-started a 6-and-5 drubbing of Love and Maggert. Faldo and Montgomerie got on the board with a 4-and-2 triumph over Haas and Strange, and in the most impressive performance, Langer and Gilford whipped Pavin and Lehman, 4 and 3.

However, back came the Americans, as they won three of the four afternoon four-ball matches in what may have been the most exciting epoch of golf Oak Hill has ever seen. Gallacher split up Faldo and Montgomerie, and each man lost with his new partner. Montgomerie went down first, as he and Torrance fell 4 and 2 to Couples and Faxon. Already 3-up through twelve, Couples turned the amphitheater that surrounds the thirteenth green into a football stadium, as his chip-in for a halving birdie sent the gallery into a frenzy. And that was only the beginning.

Rocca and Woosnam made it two for two on day two when they beat Love and Crenshaw, 3 and 2, but Haas and Mickelson gave the lead back to the United States with a 3-and-2 victory over Ballesteros and Gilford. Then Pavin and Roberts extended it to 9-7 with an epic defeat of Faldo and Langer. The match came all squared to the eighteenth, but Pavin chipped in for a winning birdie, eliciting an explosion of sound that literally shook the ground and gave Oak Hill what many folks consider to be the club's defining major tournament moment. Faxon recalled:

> *I was on the driving range with Peter Jacobsen, and Dottie Pepper was there. She had come over to watch. They had the big Jumbotron screen right there on the range, and it was funny because we could see the chip-in, and then you heard the delayed roar as the sound took a little while to travel, and it was spine-chilling. And Corey's reaction was pretty subtle, like, "I'm in such control here."*

"Corey Pavin certainly did break our hearts when he chipped in on that Saturday afternoon," Gallacher recalled. "I'll never forget that—it was one of the big moments in that Ryder Cup. That looked like the big victory and a big lead going into the singles. But I was still confident the team could do well."

Later that evening, after the singles draw had been revealed, Gallacher said, "Amateurs only think of the past; professionals think of the future." Thinking back on that phrase, Gallacher says, "I don't know where I got that from, but it sounded good at the time. Sam Torrance was in the room—he was sitting there watching a video. He had his sneakers and shorts on, a cigarette in his mouth and a Budweiser in his hand, and he said, 'You're just a poet.'"

And, as it turned out, a prophet.

A lesser team may have crumbled after Pavin's brilliant shot, but as James said, "We know that we can put out twelve players who are as good as the Americans' twelve players." The Europeans were undaunted by the sizable task ahead, and they played loose and free (not to mention wonderfully) on the last day and stole the cup.

Late Sunday afternoon, with a pall hanging over Oak Hill, Haas walked into the woods on the left side of the eighteenth fairway, consumed by the reality of what was about to happen. Needing to win the hole in order to halve his match with the unheralded Walton (which would preserve a tie and enable the Americans to retain the cup) he pull-hooked his tee shot into inescapable territory. When he found his ball and correctly surmised that he had almost no chance to make par, he knew he was about to put an exclamation point on the Americans' startling collapse.

"I couldn't have hit a worse drive if I was swinging with my eyes closed," said Haas, who had won the sixteenth and seventeenth holes to stay alive but couldn't finish the job. "I said to myself, 'This wasn't supposed to happen like this.' Our matches were supposed to be icing on the cake."

Instead, they were more like a wake, because by that time, so many of Haas's teammates had let the team down that the Europeans were already reserving a seat for the cup on the Concorde for the flight back to England. "I really didn't think they could win—I honestly thought we were too good," Strange admitted. "But that's what makes the Ryder Cup so exciting."

Ultimately, Haas didn't make par—or even bogey. When he conceded to Walton, the Europeans came spilling onto the eighteenth green in delirious glee, hugging, kissing and dousing one another with champagne in celebration of their improbable victory. "I think they [the United States] wanted to go out and bury the European team and get it over with early if they could, but it wasn't meant to be," said Paul Azinger, a former Ryder Cup team member who was at Oak Hill working as an analyst for NBC. "Under some of the most extreme pressure, the European team hit some of the most spectacular shots you'd ever want to see. People will talk about [the American] guys choking and this and that, but those [European] guys just played great."

The United States needed only five points to keep the cup, and early on that fateful Sunday, that seemed easily attainable, especially when Lehman drummed Ballesteros in the opening singles match while Love cooled off the red-hot Rocca, 3 and 2. But things began going awry when Clark and James, two Euros who hadn't played since the Friday morning foursomes, upset Jacobsen and Maggert, respectively. Couples managed a halve with Woosnam, but then Montgomerie closed out Crenshaw, and Faxon missed a six-footer at eighteen that would have provided a critical half point. Suddenly, the overall match was tied at eleven and a half apiece, with five matches on the course.

At this stage, the United States was virtually assured of two points (Mickelson was routing Johansson, and Pavin was in control against Langer), so in those final three matches, all it would need was a half point to keep possession of the cup. The United States got zero, losing all three. Torrance beat Roberts, 2 and 1, Haas lost, 1-up and Strange bogeyed the final three holes to lose to Faldo, 1-up. Strange's match is the most often recounted due to the way he crumbled and the fact that he was a captain's pick who had failed to earn even a fraction of a point in the three matches he played. Strange recalled:

> *I was a captains' pick for Lanny, and I think a lot of it had to do with the '89 Open. It was a bit controversial because he passed over a couple of players who were playing well, but they would have been rookies on a Ryder Cup team. It's a terrible ending, especially for me, finishing the way I did. I had Nick going, and I should have beaten him. I feel bad for Lanny and my teammates; they played so hard. I was in a position that I was supposed to come through in, and I didn't.*

After bogeying seventeen to allow Faldo to get even, Strange hit a perfect tee shot at eighteen, while Faldo pulled his into a dreadful lie in the left rough. All Faldo could do was chip out to the fairway and hope Strange would falter. Strange did. He hit a poor approach that landed on the bank in front of the green, and given that boost, Faldo hit a superb pitching wedge third shot from ninety-three yards away to within four feet. Strange chipped to seven feet, missed his par-saver and then watched in horror as Faldo rolled his putt dead center to win the match.

That's why it was left to Haas, but that swing at the eighteenth tee killed the final hope. "I guess that's what we all want—to be in that position—but I didn't finish it off," he said. "I figured if I could get to eighteen, I'd have the momentum, and I did, but I just hit a poor tee shot. I'll think about that one for quite awhile."

From a jingoistic standpoint, the Ryder Cup was a terrible disappointment for America, but Oak Hill was a decided victor, as it put on a first-rate show for all the world to see, prompting Bill Reeves to say to his fellow longtime member Bill Westerfeld, "Even though we lost the match, we won the world." The PGA of America took notice, too, and Oak Hill has become one of the organization's go-to venues for its major championships. It hosted the 2003 PGA and 2008 Senior PGA and in August 2013 will welcome back the PGA.

*Chapter 17*

# Ultimate Comeback

The life of Hank Kuehne could be turned into a major motion picture, or at the very least, an ESPN *30 for 30* documentary.

Alcoholic by the time he was thirteen years old? Check.

Learning disabilities as a youngster that included dyslexia, depression and attention deficit disorder? Check.

Golf prodigy and a member of one of America's most accomplished golf families who earned an athletic scholarship to Oklahoma State? Check.

Went on a drinking binge his first year in Stillwater, got behind the wheel of a car and after speeding through a stop sign crashed into another vehicle and was incredibly lucky that he, his passengers and the people in the other vehicle survived? Check.

Went to rehab, whipped his dependency on booze, re-purposed his life, enrolled at Southern Methodist University and went on to a stellar college golf career? Check.

Won the U.S. Amateur at Oak Hill Country Club? Check.

Surprisingly needed four years to earn his full-time playing privileges on the PGA Tour and enjoyed three decent years before debilitating shoulder and back injuries brought his promising career to a standstill? Check.

Had two highly publicized relationships, including a brief dalliance with singer Paula Abdul and a three-and-a-half-year stint with tennis star Venus Williams, as well as two marriages that resulted in two children? Check.

It's enough to make a supermarket tabloid cry, "Uncle!"

Fifteen years have passed since the 1998 U.S. Amateur, in which Kuehne, then twenty-two years old, wowed Oak Hill with a dynamic display of precision and power to capture the most coveted championship in amateur golf with a hard-fought 2-and-1 victory over forty-four-year-old Tom McKnight. At the time, Kuehne said it was the second-greatest victory of his life, well behind his achieving sobriety. Unfortunately for Kuehne, his Amateur victory remains the pinnacle of his golfing career, as he has never won on the PGA Tour or even the developmental tour now sponsored by Web.com. In 2013, closing in on age thirty-eight, he is still trying to make his mark.

But to his credit, through all the personal and professional peaks and valleys and all the health woes that basically robbed him of his best golfing years, Kuehne has kept a positive attitude. In 2012, when he was attempting yet another comeback, he said, "I'm a lucky guy. I have a great wife and son [his second child was born later that year], and I'm playing golf again. How can I not feel blessed?"

A near-death experience has a way of opening anyone's eyes, and for Kuehne, that moment came quite early in his Hollywood-scripted life. On that fateful February 1995 night, the thought crossed his mind that "I didn't care if I lived or died, I really didn't." However, the crash brought the blurriness of his out-of-control existence into crystal-clear focus, and he knew he needed help. "The night he had his accident, I went out myself, and I had tried to call him to come join me and my buddies, but unfortunately, he had already left. And then he got in the accident," said Hank's older brother Trip, at that time the star of Oklahoma State's golf team and who just six months earlier had lost in the finals of the 1994 U.S. Amateur to Tiger Woods. "When I got home and listened to the message on my machine, I had no idea what was going on. I didn't know if he was injured, killed or if he killed somebody. I went down there and got him out of jail, and I gave him a big hug and told him, 'I love you, but you need to get your life better. Go get better. I don't care what you have to do, just go get better.'"

Hank did, and after his life-altering stay at the Hazelden substance abuse clinic in Center City, Minnesota, he returned home to Dallas to go to school at Southern Methodist, worked as hard as he ever had on his golf game and became one of the top college players in the country.

In the summer of 1998, Kuehne hit the amateur circuit like all the top players do, and while he didn't generate great results, he felt like he was playing pretty well. And when he arrived at Oak Hill and saw how well suited the East Course was to his game, his confidence soared. "When I got there, I knew I liked the course," he said.

Interestingly, the last practice round he played before the thirty-six-hole stroke-play qualifier commenced was with McKnight. Although McKnight was nearly old enough to be his father, the two had become tight in that summer of '98, as they had been paired in several events. As they made their way around the East Course, they wondered aloud about what it would be like playing each other in the championship match. And incredibly, while there were 310 other competitors in the field, they indeed were the last 2 standing.

As has so often been the case at Oak Hill, inclement weather was a storyline, as rain interrupted play on Monday and torrential rain on Tuesday turned parts of the East and West Courses—both of which were used for the qualifier—into rivers. The qualifier wasn't completed until Wednesday, and with a thirty-six-hole total of one-under 139, Kuehne made it comfortably into the sixty-four-man match play group, as did 1997 Amateur champion Matt Kuchar, reigning British Amateur champion Sergio Garcia and other future PGA Tour pros Charles Howell, Bryce Molder, Aaron Baddeley and J.J. Henry.

Kuehne cruised through his first two matches, but when the quarterfinal pairings were set, he wasn't exactly on the radar. Nearly everyone in attendance on Friday morning—one of the largest galleries in U.S. Amateur history, according to the USGA—was out to watch Kuchar and Garcia trade blows in what had been a much-anticipated match. "It was one of the best matches I've ever played," Garcia said following his thrilling 2-and-1 victory. "It was unbelievable." Kuchar, who rallied to tie the match with a birdie at fifteen before losing the next two holes to a birdie and a par, agreed. "It was a great match, great golf, great camaraderie," he said. "I guess I ran into El Niño. It was the match of the tournament."

Kuehne dispatched Molder, 5 and 4, to advance to the semifinals, and there he rolled past Bill Lunde to secure his place in the thirty-six-hole Sunday final. McKnight joined him by defeating Sean Knapp, 5 and 3, in the quarters and Garcia, 3 and 1, in the semifinals.

Unable to come within the same area code of some of Kuehne's howitzer drives, McKnight was a decided underdog. But the petroleum distributor from Galax, Virginia, overcame Kuehne's primal scream length with a putter that was as hot as the earth's core. "I pretty much expected him to make everything he looked at," said Kuehne. McKnight nearly did, and a huge crowd estimated at 10,500 loved the drama.

With his brother Trip caddying, Hank Kuehne reached the pinnacle of his golfing career at Oak Hill.

In the morning eighteen, McKnight played his worst round of the week. He hit just four fairways and three greens, but because he needed a mere twenty-three putts, he was only 3-down at lunch. A key moment in the morning came at number seventeen when McKnight, in danger of falling 5-down, drained a thirty-footer for par to halve the hole and then won number eighteen with a par.

Carrying that momentum to the afternoon, McKnight matched a Kuehne birdie at number one by making a thirty-three-footer and then made three more birdies through number six while Kuehne hit the skids and played his poorest golf of the week. When the players stepped on the seventh tee, McKnight was 1-up, and it looked like Kuehne would be unable to recover. "You have to hope that when you have a guy 3- or 4-down that the guy uses all his momentum and everything he has to get back and pull even," said Trip Kuehne, who failed to qualify for match play and spent the rest of the week caddying for his brother. "The best thing that happened to us was Tom winning the sixth hole for him to go 1-up, because now [Hank] had to think, 'I'm down—I've got to get focused.'"

And Hank did. He hit two good shots at number seven and settled for a halve. He then caught a huge break when his wayward tee shot at number eight hit a tree and kicked into the middle of the fairway. "On eight, when the monkey there threw it out of the tree, that was pretty good to say the least," Hank said with a laugh. He eventually won that hole when McKnight three-putted for bogey to square the match, and three straight McKnight bogeys at holes ten through twelve reinstated Kuehne's 3-up lead. "Tom had putted great all day, and he finally missed a couple. So I just pretty much tried to right myself and keep knocking it on the fairway…trying to put some pressure on him," said Hank.

Another key point in the match occurred at thirteen when Kuehne answered a McKnight birdie with one of his own to maintain his lead. And after McKnight won fourteen and fifteen to get within 1-down, Kuehne responded like the champion he was about to become. He made a clutch six-foot slider for par to halve sixteen and then hit a monster drive and solid pitching wedge (yes, a pitching wedge) at the long par-four seventeenth to set up a winning par. "There was a lot of emotion out there all day for both of us," said McKnight. "There were peaks and valleys all day. I didn't play my best at times, but I made up for it with some great saves. I'm happy as can be for [Hank], and I'm disappointed as hell for me."

Trip experienced similar feelings:

> *It was tears for Tom, because I know what he'll be going through. There were tears for 1994 and how close I was, but most of my tears were tears of joy for my little brother, who finally got a break in life. For all practical purposes, he was alive, but he was dead* [prior to the accident]. *To get from there to the top of the golf world in a matter of three years was a pretty big accomplishment.*

On that day when Hank raised the Havemeyer Trophy over his head in triumph, he had no idea that there would be so many struggles still ahead for him. All he knew is that he'd already been through so much, and no matter what the future held, he would be able to meet the challenges head on. "I feel I'm one of the luckiest people to be alive," Kuehne said that week. "I've been through a car wreck—almost died. I've had a lot of things go bad, and the thing is, I learned more about myself going through that experience than the majority of people learn in a lifetime—and I learned it at nineteen."

Five years later, when Kuehne returned to Oak Hill to play in the 2003 PGA Championship, he reflected further on his journey, saying:

> *I wouldn't be alive if I wasn't sober. Without my sobriety, I wouldn't have had the opportunity to be there* [at Oak Hill]. *There were points when I was so low in my life, and then at that moment, it doesn't seem like anything had ever been bad. That was a great victory, and it's one of the things I'm most proud of in my golf career. But then again, it's still second. I could win ten majors or five majors or something like that, but there's nothing I can do in this game that would ever surpass my sobriety.*

## *Chapter 18*

# Premier Service

At most golf facilities or country clubs, whether they are private or public, the head professional is often the most recognizable face on the staff. But a club as grandiose as Oak Hill relies on so many other employees to make sure the members and their guests are treated to as fine an experience as possible. Inside the clubhouse, the roster of Oak Hill's general managers—the men and women who have run the hospitality side of the operation—is every bit as impressive as those who have stood sentry in the pro shop.

Craig Harmon has a tree dedicated to him on the Hill of Fame, but it's unlikely that many folks (at least those who aren't members) know that one of the most beautiful trees on the property, the weeping beech that stands regally in front of the entrance to the clubhouse, is appropriately dedicated to one of Oak Hill's most influential former employees, the late Ruth McKinnon. McKinnon worked as a secretary at Oak Hill for five years before being promoted to club manager in 1933, making her the first woman in the nation to hold that position at such a large and prestigious country club.

"To have to handle this number of people…this is a big job," former club president Allen Brewer once said of McKinnon, who held that position for nineteen years. McKinnon helped guide the club through the World War II years and its first hosting of a major tournament, the 1949 U.S. Amateur, for which she was honored by the U.S. Golf Association for outstanding service.

Upon leaving Oak Hill, McKinnon started her own restaurant in Rochester, led the Monroe County Unit of the American Cancer Society and headed the civil defense emergency feeding program for Monroe County.

Ruth McKinnon was the first female in the country to hold the position of manager at a private country club, and she ran the clubhouse operation for nineteen years.

A graduate of East High and the Rochester Business Institute, McKinnon passed away in 1994. Her niece, Pip Powell of Pittsford, said at the time, "She was always for the underdog, even in the golf tournaments. My aunt was a super lady." Oak Hill knew this.

Joe Brem came to Oak Hill to serve as general manager in 1961 after stints at Brook-Lea Country Club in Rochester and Niagara Falls Country Club, and in the near decade that he served, yearly food sales more than doubled. Brem knew the business, and he was well known for always putting the betterment of the club and its social environment first.

Jack Thomas joined the club in 1972, the year head pro Craig Harmon did, and he brought stability and a smiling face to the position for the next seventeen years. As longtime club secretary Norma Heinlein once said, "Everyone loved him." A graduate of Cornell, Thomas worked at several clubs for a period of eighteen years before coming to Oak Hill, where he was credited with establishing the club's unparalleled organizational structure that remains largely in place today.

Eric Rule was the longest-tenured general manager in club history, holding that position for twenty-three years.

Eric Rule assumed the position when Thomas retired following the 1989 U.S. Open, and having worked under Thomas since 1985, he was more than ready to ascend to the main office. Rule enjoyed a magnificent twenty-three-year career before leaving Oak Hill in 2012, during which the club enjoyed unprecedented growth and financial success.

No Oak Hill general manager presided over more major tournaments than Rule, and he kept the club humming along during some of its biggest infrastructural projects, including the magnificent renovations of the clubhouse, the addition of a state-of-the-art fitness center, a new outdoor patio and the creation and building of the Oak Hill Museum.

And then there are the men who have been tasked with maintaining the world-renowned East Course and the often-overlooked West Course. Having to take care of a single eighteen-hole layout is more than enough work, as any greens superintendent will tell you, so imagine what it's like to groom thirty-six holes, half of which are occasionally on display for all the world to see when Oak Hill hosts a major event. If ever there was a man born to do this job, it was Elmer Michael. Michael's father, Charles, began working as greens superintendent at the Country Club of Buffalo when Elmer was an infant and later worked at Park Country Club outside Buffalo and Brook-Lea.

After learning at the elbow of his father, Elmer went on to spend forty-three years in the business, coming to Oak Hill in 1929, when the Donald Ross courses were only three years old and in desperate need of nurturing. He played a key role in Dr. Williams's landscape and tree-planting program, oversaw the installation of the fairway irrigation

Elmer Michaels was the greens superintendent at Oak Hill for more than thirty-five years.

system (which was the first of its kind in the country) and helped rebuild bunkers and tees under the direction of architect Robert Trent Jones Sr. prior to the 1956 U.S. Open.

Michaels's assistant, Lynn Kellogg, replaced him in 1966 and helped perform the work on the new par-three hole that was built for the 1968 U.S. Open.

Joseph Baidy, who later in his career served as president of the Golf Course Superintendents Association, came to Oak Hill in 1970. Baidy helped the club through two major incidents: the flood of 1972, which ravaged many Mid-Atlantic states and was particularly damaging to the Southern Tier of New York, and the Pure Waters District interceptor sewer line project that had to be laid out underneath portions of the East Course.

Dick Bator was hired in 1978 and had to nurse the East Course through the controversial renovation in the mid- to late 1970s to ready it for the 1980 PGA Championship. In addition to the changes on the front nine in the congested area where the fifth and sixth holes come together, he built three new tees and laid three miles of drainage lines for that tournament. He worked at Oak Hill for a mere five years, but he was a valued consultant long thereafter.

Joe Hahn has the distinction of having worked during the most major events, as he was in charge of the preparation and maintenance for the 1984 U.S. Senior Open, the 1989 U.S. Open, the 1995 Ryder Cup and the 1998 U.S. Amateur. His work during the '89 Open, during which torrential overnight rains between the second and third rounds threatened to ruin the tournament, was regarded as legendary in his field. Through the tireless work of Hahn and his crew, the tournament continued with barely a hitch, which seemed impossible on that Saturday morning when he arrived at the course and discovered several new water hazards.

Hahn also oversaw the vitally important transformation of the greens from South German bent grass, which had been in place since Ross sculpted the courses and had been overrun by *Poa annua*, to Providence bent grass prior to the Ryder Cup. Seeing the greens on the East Course burned to a crisp in August 1993 was certainly a jarring sight for the membership, but once the new surfaces were ready for play, it became obvious how necessary the project had been, and Hahn's foresight was lauded.

Paul Latshaw, who had been the head super at Merion Golf Club and had also worked as an assistant at three of the most historic courses in the country—Augusta National, Oakmont and Pine Valley—came to Oak Hill in 1999 to replace Hahn. Latshaw, whose father, Paul Sr., was a well-known superintendent who worked at several places including Oakmont and Congressional, was instrumental in the 2001 installation of a state-of-the-art irrigation system, as well as nearly $1 million in drainage upgrades that included about seven miles of new pipe and new tiles under approximately 75 percent of the bunkers.

It can be argued that the East Course was never better than it was for the 2003 PGA, and *Golf Digest* took notice in its annual ranking of the top

Joe Hahn prepared the East Course for four major tournaments during his sixteen years with the club.

courses in America. In 1993, with the Ryder Cup two years away from fruition and the old greens still in place, the East Course sat fifteenth on the list. By 1999, it had slipped to twenty-sixth. But on the heels of these latest renovations, Oak Hill leaped to number ten, and in the breakdown of particular categories, it ranked tied for second in course condition with Augusta National behind only the Quarry at La Quinta, a new course in the California desert. "It's quite a thrill," then–Oak Hill president Doug Weins said at that time. "It's a culmination of four years worth of work. On a personal level, words can't describe the excitement. I'm so excited for Oak Hill and the membership."

Latshaw worked through the 2003 PGA Championship before leaving Oak Hill to take the superintendents' job at Jack Nicklaus's Muirfield Village in Dublin, Ohio. Since his departure, the courses have been in the capable hands of Jeff Corcoran, who had interned under Hahn in 1994 and was the head man at Weston Golf Club in Massachusetts before returning to Oak Hill in 2003.

With the East Course in peak condition, thanks to all the attention paid to it for the PGA Championship, Corcoran's first order of business was to "put a lot more attention into the West Course and make sure there was parity

Jeff Corcoran has been the greens superintendent at Oak Hill since October 2003.

between the two golf courses." Corcoran oversaw the renovation of greens and bunkers, the re-paving of cart paths and the installation of a new irrigation system.

Corcoran met another big challenge with the 2008 Senior PGA during Memorial Day weekend, which was the earliest Oak Hill had ever hosted a major tournament. Corcoran and his crew overcame different grass growing and foliage conditions and frosty temperatures on the first day of competition, and there was nary a worry, as the course was in its usual pristine condition.

## *Chapter 19*

# GLORY'S LAST SHOT

It was nearly an hour after Shaun Micheel had executed the shot of his life (perhaps the shot of the 2003 golf season) and certainly the shot that secured his unlikely triumph in the PGA Championship at Oak Hill, and the magnitude of it all still hadn't yet registered.

So it was no surprise that as Micheel stared out at the horde of reporters inquiring how in the world he had hit a pressure-packed 7-iron from 175 yards at the seventy-second hole to within two inches of the cup, thus slamming the door on persistent runner-up Chad Campbell, he seemed a bit flabbergasted. "I can't really believe that this happened to me," said the then thirty-four-year-old from Memphis as he stole a glance at the elegant Wanamaker Trophy glistening under the spotlights right next to him.

Quite frankly, neither could anyone else in that interview room, any of the more than thirty-five thousand spectators who roared their approval at Oak Hill on that Sunday afternoon ten years ago or the millions who were watching the CBS Sports broadcast worldwide.

On a historic old course, where the list of winners of past major championships included the likes of Cary Middlecoff, Lee Trevino, Jack Nicklaus and Curtis Strange—not to mention non-major event winners Ben Hogan and Sam Snead—who could blame anyone for scratching their heads and wondering aloud, "Who is Shaun Micheel, and how did he win the PGA Championship?" His name didn't exactly roll off the tongue with the same reverence, but the names that would have—Tiger Woods, Phil Mickelson, Mike Weir, Jim Furyk, Vijay Singh, Fred Couples, Ernie Els and Rochester's own favorite son, Jeff Sluman—were getting swallowed by Oak Hill's gnarly rough, so somebody had to win. Nondescript as he was, Micheel turned out to be that man. And while virtually no one in golf fandom knew who he was even as recently as two days earlier when he soared into contention, he deserved it.

Micheel's gritty final-round even-par 70 gave him a four-under total of 276, two strokes clear of Campbell (72-278), and made it a clean sweep for first-time winners in the 2003 majors (a month earlier, Ben Curtis had won the British Open), something that hadn't happened since 1969, the year Micheel was born.

Of course, that meant that Woods went a year without winning a major for the first time since 1998. And following his inaugural competitive appearance at Oak Hill, while Micheel was being feted, Tiger humbly left town with his tail between his legs, knowing he'd been beaten not so much by Micheel but by a magnificent golf course.

Tiger Woods didn't play well, but he had nothing but praise for Oak Hill.

Woods finished the tournament tied for thirty-ninth place with a twelve-over-par total of 292, to that point his worst score in relation to par in a major as a professional. And it was only the third time he had failed to beat par in all four rounds. But Woods had nothing to complain about, as he called Oak Hill the toughest, fairest course he'd ever played. Still, he was happy when his miserable week was finished. "It was a tough week," he said. "I fought hard just to shoot bad."

As surprising as Tiger's struggles were, nothing could match the disbelief in the gallery over the fact that Micheel had won the tournament. Given that

Curtis had entered the British Open at Royal St. George's as the 396th-ranked player in the world and came away victorious, Micheel wasn't nearly as much of a long shot, as he had begun his week at Oak Hill ranked 169th. However, Micheel had been winless in 163 PGA Tour career starts, had won only two tournaments as a pro—one each on the Nike Tour (1999) and the Asian Tour (1998)—and had come to Oak Hill with just three top-ten finishes in 22 starts in 2003. Odds were that you couldn't get odds on Micheel, and if he were a betting man, he wouldn't have wagered a dime on himself. "I showed up here Tuesday to play a practice round, and when I saw how difficult this golf course was, I was just trying to make the cut," he said. "That was my main goal, and I probably would have been happy with that."

Micheel wasn't alone. Most of the field recognized how challenging Oak Hill was going to be. A stretch of rain leading up to the start of the tournament had sent the lush rough into overdrive, and the grounds crew could barely keep pace. There were spots on the course where it was so long that it didn't stand up straight; it just laid over, and if you drew a lie that was going against the grain, you were cooked. All week, unless players caught a lucky break, if they drove the ball into the rough, they were likely just wedging back to the fairway and hoping to one-putt for pars—U.S. Open style.

There was plenty of buzz on the first day when Mickelson, then still in search of his first major championship, opened with a four-under 66, which matched his career-best PGA Championship round and was eight strokes better than Woods's 74. "I thought that I did a number of things well," said Mickelson, who made six birdies and two bogeys to share the lead with Australian Rod Pampling, one stroke better than Billy Andrade. "It was a nice start, but it's nothing more than that."

Mickelson raised a few eyebrows when he opined that he didn't think the course was too hard, a statement that came back to bite him. "He started out like a ball of fire. I think he was three- or four-under after seven or eight holes—something like that," Sluman recalled. "But Oak Hill always has a way of getting back at you."

Sluman was right. The course had begun drying out, and it was already starting to become more difficult to stop slightly off-kilter shots from bounding into the jungle-like rough. On the second day, this was a problem for many in the field, including Mickelson, who found nothing easy about the layout and ballooned to a 75.

But while some of the world's best players struggled, Micheel introduced himself to the golf world by making birdies on four of his last five holes for a two-under 68 that was the best on a brutally tough scoring day. "This is only my third major championship," said Micheel. "Players rate their careers on how many majors they've won. Heck, I've only played in three, so I was just really happy and honored to be invited."

After Strange became the first man since Ben Hogan to win back-to-back U.S. Opens when he won at Oak Hill in 1989, he said, "Move over, Ben." Micheel served notice that by the end of the week, he might be saying the same thing—only his reference would be to Ben Curtis, whom he would supplant as the most recent longest of long shots to win a major. His 68, one of only five sub-par rounds on Friday, gave him a two-shot cushion on Andrade. "I think it shows that the comments a week ago that I was hearing that the golf course might not be difficult enough and might not hold up were a little off," said Sluman, who suffered through a gruesome two rounds, shooting 75-79 to miss the cut in his second major championship appearance on his home course.

"If it gets any tougher, it's almost going to be unfair," said Davis Love III, the Tour's leading money winner heading into the week who also missed the cut. Said Els, who shot 70 and was four shots in arrears, "It could be one of the toughest ever. It's not as long as Bethpage [site of the 2002 U.S. Open], but it definitely has the rough. Already we have seen the greens firm up a little bit, so it will be tough to go under par. There is no question about this golf course maybe being too easy."

However, it was a little easier on Saturday, as the rough received a much-needed trim while overnight rain softened the fairways and greens. Micheel pounced on that opportunity early and actually got to seven-under. Only Nicklaus had ever gone that low during any of the majors at Oak Hill, and he was there for only two holes in the third round of the 1980 PGA. At that point, Micheel held a four-stroke lead, but just when it seemed like he was in control, he bogeyed the final three holes and settled for a 69 that left him at four-under 206, tied for the top spot with Campbell, who pieced together a scorching 65, just one shot off the competitive course record shared by Strange and Hogan. "What a disappointing finish," said Micheel, which was not something Campbell concurred with. Campbell made six birdies against a lone bogey at the brutally hard seventeenth hole and remarked, "I felt really good out there. I hit a lot of fairways and greens and gave myself a lot of opportunities for birdie. I had quite a few putts that I didn't take advantage of, putts that were definitely makeable. It was nice to get a few at the end and kind of make up for that."

As play began on the final day, it was assumed that the one player still in the hunt who could throw a scare into Micheel and Campbell was Weir, the left-handed Canadian who'd broken through at Augusta four months earlier. Instead, his three-shot deficit more than doubled within the first hour of his round, as the 2003 Player of the Year candidate bogeyed the first five holes.

Micheel started well with a birdie at number one, but by the time he made the turn after bogeys at holes seven and eight, he was wobbling at three-under for the tournament and was tied for the lead with Tim Clark of South Africa, who went three-under on the front side. Campbell played the first nine in three-over, but when Clark began to fade, Campbell regrouped and regained the drafting position behind Micheel with a birdie at the par-five thirteenth, setting up a frenetic dash to the wire.

Micheel enjoyed a two-shot swing at the short par-four fourteenth when he drove the green and two-putted for birdie while Campbell bogeyed, but he gave those back at the par-three fifteenth when he three-putted for bogey and Campbell drained a twenty-five-foot roller coaster of a putt for birdie. Micheel answered with a thirty-foot birdie at sixteen after a strong wedge out of the cabbage to the right of the fairway, but then he missed another drive at seventeen and settled for a bogey, cutting his lead back to one as they strode to the home hole.

Here, the golf gods repaid Micheel for all the struggles he had endured in eleven years on the pro tours. He pulled his drive at eighteen, but when it landed, it thumped into a mound on the edge of the fairway. Instead of bounding into the primary rough, the ball squirted right and stopped in the barely penal first cut. "From what it looked from the tee, it got a pretty nice bounce," said Micheel.

And then he struck an absolutely perfect shot. "Normally, you see guys waffling back and forth between clubs," Micheel said. "I had the yardage that my caddie mentioned [a similar shot hit in a practice round] on Tuesday that we had, and I hit. When that ball was in the air, all I was asking for was just to carry to the front of the green."

As usual, the golf ball did not listen, but this was a good thing, as it didn't just carry the front edge, it hopped back to the pin and stopped a couple of rolls from the hole. The ball was majestic in flight against the backdrop of the jam-packed grandstands—grandstands that nearly collapsed in excitement when the ball nearly tumbled in for a *Tin Cup* finish. "That would probably be the best shot I've seen under pressure," said Campbell, who hit a pretty good one himself at eighteen and settled for a par to secure a solo runner-up finish.

"It's kind of scary, really," Micheel said with a look of honest-to-goodness awe on his face. "I was trying to win the BC Open a year ago at this time [he blew a three-shot lead on the final day and lost]. Even up until maybe a month or two ago, I was trying to keep my card. To have my name on that trophy…I don't know what I'm thinking right now. I look down that list right there [on the trophy] and see all the names, and I just hope that maybe I can produce a career like a lot of those guys have."

Unfortunately, he hasn't come close. Heading into 2013, Micheel had not won another tournament, and he had just eleven top-ten finishes since his victory at Oak Hill, one of those being a runner-up to Woods in the 2006 PGA Championship. It has been a struggle that included a serious shoulder injury, the death of his mother, a lawsuit that was settled out of court against his former agent and a battle with the PGA Tour regarding its anti-doping policy and his use of a banned substance to treat low testosterone, a condition that had been diagnosed three years before the tour began drug testing in 2008.

There have been plenty of down times, but Micheel will always have his glorious moment at Oak Hill. "I watch it quite often," he said of the DVD he has of the broadcast. "I need that sometimes. It was exciting and something that I'll remember for the rest of my life."

*Chapter 20*

# REDEMPTION

The day after it happened, Jay Haas certainly wasn't thinking that he had just learned a valuable lesson, one that would help him for the rest of his professional golf career. The day after the Ryder Cup left Greater Rochester International Airport and flew back to Europe in late September 1995, there was no slapping a smiley face on the admittedly horrendous tee shot he struck during his singles match against Europe's Philip Walton. It was a shot that had played a pivotal role in the United States' demise that fateful afternoon.

As Haas packed his bags at the Woodcliff Hotel for his own flight home, that Monday was a time for remorse, for mourning, for feeling sick to your stomach and for understanding that as long as he continued to play this crazy game of golf, he was never going to forget that shot.

That was a tough day indeed, but then came Tuesday, and Haas started to fight back. He concluded that the only way he was going to be able to deal with the disappointment of what happened at Oak Hill, aptly nicknamed Heartbreak Hill, was to look for something positive to take from one of the most disheartening experiences of his life. "I think back to that drive a lot when I get into a pressure situation and I say, 'You know, trying to fit this drive into the fairway isn't the answer,'" Haas said thirteen years later when he was back at Oak Hill and preparing to play in the 2008 Senior PGA Championship. He continued:

> *I won't say it's one of the best things that ever happened to me, but since then I've thought about it, and I realized that I was trying to be too perfect on that drive. I was trying to collect myself and all that rigmarole that I thought was the proper thing to do, when in fact, I needed my instincts to take over and just rip it. Now I pick a shot and commit to it, because I wasn't committed to that shot at that time. That has been somewhat of a turnaround for me mentally—to commit to a shot a little better.*

Haas remembered not only the physical failure but also the mental letdown that occurred on that pull hook that killed any chance he had of defeating Walton and enabling the United States to retain the cup. "I don't know that I was totally mentally prepared to be the guy coming down the stretch," he said. "It was the eleventh match out of twelve, and I didn't think my point would really matter one way or the other. I've choked countless times out here, and we all have to a certain point, but that was one of my greatest where I didn't do what I was trained to do. I don't want that again, and since then I've just felt that I'd rather go down in flames than go down whimpering."

And so, as he came to that same eighteenth hole less than a week after sharing those thoughts, needing to stripe one down the middle and make a par to win the Senior PGA, Haas purposely thought back to 1995 and challenged himself to make amends—if not to his teammates, then at least to his own psyche. "I was definitely thinking of that," Haas said.

Clinging to a precarious one-stroke lead over Bernhard Langer when he pushed his tee into the ground at the 469-yard eighteenth, Haas thought about the mental makeover he made after the Ryder Cup and basically told himself, "Well, you've been talking about this, so it's time to put up or shut up. You talked a good game about just getting up there and ripping it and all that stuff. And damned if I didn't do it."

His shot soared safely down the left-center of the fairway, and then he hit a 6-iron to within about seventeen feet of the flag. Two putts later, Haas had not only won the Senior PGA for the second time in three years but had also clearly exorcised his eighteenth-hole demons at Oak Hill. "I was thinking that I was trying to get to eighteen with a three- or four-shot lead so I wouldn't have to think about it," he said, laughing at the thought. "But I think that might make it even sweeter—the fact that I just had a one-shot lead."

There were many outcomes that would have made this a wonderful tournament, not the least of which was Rochester's own Jeff Sluman not only making the cut on his home course in a major event but also winning in front of his adoring fans. But Haas coming through in the clutch on a course that he truly loved despite what had happened in 1995 was certainly a popular result.

Only Haas, Arnold Palmer and Billy Casper have teed it up in five major tournaments at Oak Hill, but Haas's connection to Oak Hill goes beyond his number of starts. "We were talking on the way in about how many memories I have here—even more than tour stops, where I played twenty-five years in a row," Haas said. "I have so many things that stand out in my head…some golf stuff, but a lot of off-the-course stuff, too."

Haas's longtime caddie on the regular tour was Billy Harmon, brother of Oak Hill head pro Craig Harmon, who would be on his bag for this tournament. Whenever Haas came to Rochester, be it for the 1980 PGA, the 1989 U.S. Open, the '95 Ryder Cup, the '03 PGA or the '08 Senior PGA, he spent quality time with the Harmon family, and those are recollections that he cherishes. "He said he's never had a club where he's had more diverse memories," Billy Harmon said. "And he loves the golf course."

For only the second time, Oak Hill hosted a senior major championship, and just like the first, when Miller Barber outdueled Palmer to win the 1984 U.S. Senior Open, the Senior PGA did not lack in drama. The show was every bit as exciting and compelling as any of the other major tournaments. One of the reasons for this is Rochester's legendary appreciation for the game and its history. As exciting as it was to have young guns Tiger Woods and Phil Mickelson and the rest of the long-hitting PGA Tour stars in town for the 2003 PGA, the names on the starters' sheet for the Senior PGA read like a who's who of legends—players that the vast majority of those in attendance watched every week on television in the 1970s and '80s. There was Haas and Langer; Sluman and the other local favorite, Horseheads native Joey Sindelar; Greg Norman; Tom Watson; Craig Stadler; Ian Woosnam; Loren Roberts; Mark O'Meara; Fuzzy Zoeller; and Hale Irwin among the biggest names, as well as dozens of others who had played in previous majors at Oak Hill and made nice livings on the regular tour before joining the fifty-and-above Champions Tour.

And while Rochester was thrilled that this event was at Oak Hill as part of a two-for-one deal with the PGA of America that also included the 2013 PGA Championship, the players who knew and loved the classic beauty and challenge of the East Course were just as pumped up to be back. "I can tell you that I know our players are excited about it," Rick George, president of the Champions Tour, said regarding Oak Hill. "We think it's a great venue to host a major championship. The PGA of America works pretty hard in identifying the best places around the country to host the championship, so we're pretty enthusiastic about that venue and what it offers."

Haas provided an early indication that it might be his week when he opened the tournament with a one-under 69, the lone score in the 60s on a cold, raw un-spring-like day. The morning wind-chill factor was in the high thirties, and those in attendance looked like they should have been walking to their seats at the often-frigid home of the Buffalo Bills, Ralph Wilson Stadium, instead of down the first fairway in pursuit of Sluman and his playing partners, Norman and Zoeller. Rain fell for about the first hour, and then the wind began to blow, and while it wasn't consistently fierce, it certainly had its moments. The wind, the wetness and temperatures that never exceeded the low fifties conspired to exact a heavy toll on the 155-man field that, by and large, was no longer equipped to excel in those conditions.

Sluman, who managed a 70 to draft just one stroke behind Haas, quipped that he hit a 3-wood on the first tee "off the snow," and it was only a little white lie. And Norman, who shot 72, said, "It was tough to get the body going. I'm not used to swinging with four layers of clothes on, so it was a tough day."

Haas made three bogeys in his round, predicting that there were more of those to come, as he thought it was "the hardest set-up for a major tournament on the Champions Tour that I've played."

The second round saw seven players break par, including Haas's good buddy, Tom Purtzer, who played in the group ahead of Haas and shot a 67 that vaulted him into the midway lead. "It looked like he was playing really well," Haas said. "It looked like it was an easy day for him."

Well, that may have been a bit of an overstatement, because there was nothing easy about the East Course this week. And Purtzer was quick to announce that even though he shot three-under for an even-par total of 140, one better than Haas (72-141) and Massy Kuramoto (68-141), he wouldn't mind if the Oak Hill grounds crew fired up the lawnmowers and scaled back the rough a couple of inches.

"We always say that the Open is the hardest setup, but the way the golf course is here, it's every bit as tough as a U.S. Open," said Purtzer, who shook his head at the cut figure of twelve-over, highest for a Senior PGA since 1990. "Usually, the PGA is friendlier to us than the USGA. But not this week. It's borderline too tough. I mean it's really brutal. I just feel fortunate to be here."

On a gloriously sunny Saturday, Sluman was feeling pretty fortunate, too. The hometown hero had endured heartbreak and frustration in his other two starts at Oak Hill in the '89 Open and '03 PGA, failing to make the cut in both. However, rounds of 70 and 73 qualified him for the weekend, and then, during the third round, he put together another 70 and climbed all the way into a second-place tie with Haas, one stroke behind Langer. This meant that the three would play together in the final threesome Sunday. "I'd like a ten-shot lead—that's the scenario that I would really like," Sluman said with a smile that cracked up the media room. "It's going to be great tomorrow. Last group for me with Jay, especially being a very close friend, and I think the golf is going to be terrific. I know the people are going to come out, and whoever wins is going to play some terrific golf."

Greece's Jeff Sluman played in the final group on Sunday but struggled to a 78 and finished four shots behind Jay Haas.

Purtzer disappeared quickly as he played the front nine in seven-over, ultimately shooting 81 on a day when once again, only one player—Scott Simpson with a 69—broke par. While Purtzer was flaming, Sluman was doing what he'd always dreamed—eliciting guttural roars from his hometown. "Certainly it was a great day," said Sluman. "I played very well today, and I thought I did what I obviously set out to do."

Sluman and Langer went back and forth all afternoon, and when they matched twos at the par-three fifteenth, Sluman had five birdies on his card, and he and Langer were tied for the lead at even par. They both bogeyed sixteen and seventeen, and then at eighteen, Sluman found the rough for the third straight hole, wedged into the fairway, wedged onto the green and missed an eight-footer for par. Langer bested him, as he got up and down for par from the hill in front of the green to grab the lead heading into the fourth round. "We both hit the ball very well, and it was just fun being out there," said Langer. "It was a great atmosphere—the people really got into it. I noticed that he's obviously the hometown boy here. People took a liking to him, and they just treat him very special."

For a while, it looked as if Sluman and Langer were going to create some separation from the rest of the pack, but that all changed in a head-spinning span of about three minutes. During that time, Sluman and Langer made their bogeys at seventeen, and just as Sluman was teeing off at eighteen, Haas holed out a 162-yard 8-iron shot from the left rough at seventeen for an eagle that seemingly served as a warning shot for what was to come on Sunday. It vaulted him into a three-way tie for the lead, but like Sluman, he bogeyed eighteen to slip a stroke behind Langer.

Haas was middling along and was four-over-par through ten holes, unable to hole anything and five shots out of the lead. But then came a birdie at fifteen, a par at sixteen and the shot of the tournament at seventeen. And all of a sudden, he was right back in the mix. "It was a pretty amazing turn of events," he said. "I'm thrilled to be one of those three. Jeff's one of my best buddies out here, and I enjoy watching Bernhard compete. I couldn't ask for a better group on Sunday."

And he sure couldn't have asked for a better result, as he outlasted those two with a hard-fought-if-not-artistic 74 that gave him a seven-over 287, the highest winning seventy-two-hole score in Oak Hill history. The carnage for the final threesome (who played the round in a cumulative 18-over-par) began on the first hole when Langer double-bogeyed, Sluman bogeyed and Haas made a par that gave him a lead he never relinquished.

Things never got better for Sluman. It simply wasn't his day, and he knew "after a couple holes, four or five," that it was going to be a long, tough day. After the bogey at number one, he made three more on the front and then had two bogeys and a killer double-bogey (at fifteen) on the back while never making a birdie, closing out a disappointing 78, dropping him into a tie for ninth.

"I guess all I can say is that I'm glad it wasn't a five-round tournament; it would be a TKO right now," said Sluman, who hit just four of fourteen fairways Sunday. "This golf course kicks your butt when you drive it and hit it where I did."

Langer bounced back from a gruesome front-nine 41, and after he made birdie at eleven and Haas bogeyed thirteen, the lead was down to one. From then on, it became a match-play situation. The two matched pars at fourteen, fifteen and sixteen, and each made a bogey at seventeen. And then came the drama at eighteen—the moment when Haas summoned the memory of the Ryder Cup and used it to his advantage.

Langer drove into the first cut of rough on the right and then hit a 5-iron that was pushed right by the wind and finished sixty feet from the hole. After Haas hit his perfect tee shot and reached the green safely, he watched as Langer gave his putt a great ride only to narrowly miss and settle for par. Haas missed his birdie attempt but then made a knee-knocking two-footer to secure the championship.

"I probably made one of my most solid pars I've ever made with two of my best shots under pressure, and that's what I'm leaving here with," he said. "With the trophy and the thought of doing that under the gun. I feel pretty happy about that. It's such a great place. I enjoy the town of Rochester, and this is one of my top-five favorite courses. Most of it is all good here, except for the '95 Ryder Cup."

*Chapter 21*

# Oak Hill in 2013 and Beyond

Tiger Woods has played only one tournament at Oak Hill, the 2003 PGA Championship, and though it was one of his worst scoring weeks in a major championship, he drove off in his rental car, several hours before out-of-nowhere winner Shaun Micheel hit the clinching shot at the seventy-second hole, without a hint of anger. Woods is not a happy-go-lucky loser. But he knew Oak Hill's East Course whipped him fair and square, and he was OK with that. After the final round, he said:

> *This is the hardest, fairest golf course I've ever played. It's not tricked up; it's right there in front of you. It's just very difficult. If you drive the ball in play, you can go ahead and shoot a good number. But if you are not getting it in play, it's going to be a tough week. It's a lot of fun to play golf courses that are fair and challenging at the same time.*

Which is why the PGA of America fully expects to be holding more of its championship events at Oak Hill in the years to come.

"I would say it's no secret that we feel this is a special place, the relationship we have with Oak Hill is second to none," said Pete Bevacqua, the chief executive officer of the PGA of America. "We have a lot of great relationships but I can't imagine a scenario that we wouldn't come back. The course deserves it, the community deserves it, and it's one of the great historic venues. You can go around and count on two hands the number of courses around

The PGA of America will be bringing the PGA Championship to Oak Hill for the third time in 2013.

this country that were competitive to the level that they could host the best players in the early twentieth century and then in 2013."

Kerry Haigh, the PGA of America's chief championship officer who for nearly two decades has been in charge of setting up the courses for the association's major events, the 2013 PGA being his fourth at Oak Hill, added, "I think it will sustain for years because it's a great golf course, and it has always proved to be a great test. Anytime you come to a course with the history that this venue has…it's wonderful. The players enjoy the test that it brings, and we enjoy setting it up. We've had an outstanding relationship with Oak Hill. We're really looking forward to this being a great championship, and there's no reason why we won't continue to be a part of Oak Hill's history in the future."

In Woods's early years, when he took the PGA Tour by storm and began his quest to surpass Jack Nicklaus as the most prolific major championship winner in history, many courses (most notably Augusta National, home of the Masters) tried to "Tiger-proof" their layout in an attempt to counter his otherworldly length. Oak Hill has never needed to be "Tiger-proofed."

As more and more of America's classic courses are becoming overmatched by the modern game, Oak Hill has stood up to the challenge, primarily because its diligent membership has remained proactive when renovations have been deemed necessary. And because of well-thought-out and intelligent planning followed by meticulous execution, the changes that have been made through the years have kept Oak Hill relevant nearly ninety years since it relocated to Pittsford. In fact, they have actually enhanced an already near-flawless layout. "It's a testament to this place that it has stood up to the test of time—all the way back to the 1949 Amateur," said Jeff Corcoran, the greens superintendent since 2003. "I think it's going to be relevant again in 2013 and well into the future."

When Woods and the best players in the world return for the ninety-fifth PGA Championship, the only thing they will find appreciably different are the remodeled greens at numbers five, six and fifteen. And they should be pleased, because all three surfaces were regraded with less severe slopes in order to give more advantageous areas for pin placements.

"Those greens have historically been the ones that have been most criticized," Corcoran said, adding number eighteen to the conversation even though that green was not altered. "With today's green speeds and the slope on those greens, we needed cupping spaces, and we didn't have many options because of the slopes." That work was performed in 2010, and the members are thrilled with the results, even though the fifteenth, with the pond lurking ever so ominously just a few feet from the right edge of the putting surface, has become a tougher hole.

"We had to blow that green up and start from scratch," said Corcoran. "We tried to keep the same design characteristics, but we had to change that green enough to create more cupping area and still bring the pond more into play. In the 2013 PGA, I think fifteen is going to play very difficult."

Beyond the three new greens, the East Course will look and feel very similar to the layout that brought the best in the game to their knees in 2003, when only three players finished under par for seventy-two holes, none of whom were named Woods, Mickelson, Els or Singh.

The fifth green of the East Course being rebuilt in 2010.

The fifteenth green of the East Course gets a complete makeover.

No new tees have been built, so the course will play just a tad north of seven thousand yards, right around where it was for both the 2003 PGA and the 2008 Senior PGA. The bunkers have been uniformly groomed, some of the fairways have been slightly narrowed and numerous trees have been removed as part of an ongoing strategy started in the mid-1990s to help allow for better airflow and more sunlight for the health of the greens, a project that has been accomplished without lessening shot values. "It's such a wonderful golf course, and it's one that you don't have to keep changing, because it's so good already," Haigh said. "It's going to be a wonderful test, and the only thing we are looking to adjust is the height of the rough and whether we're going to grade the rough."

Oh yes, the rough. That's something the players will be very interested in as they begin to arrive on site. A classic old-school course like Oak Hill has three primary defenses against the modern player who can hit 360-yard drives with souped-up, twenty-first-century equipment: its abundance of trees, its speedy and sloped greens and the length and lushness of its rough. And in 2003, the rough came out as the overwhelming champion.

Because of some ill-timed rain leading up to the start of the event, the grounds crew—then led by Paul Latshaw—wasn't able to get out and properly groom the rough, making it borderline unplayable in some areas. If a player missed a fairway, he was lucky to find the ball let alone hit a quality shot. Many spectators and media folks felt that the severity of the rough sapped some excitement from the tournament because in most cases, the only option wayward drivers had was to wedge the ball back into play and then try to make one-putt pars. There weren't a whole lot of birdies, and while that's not necessarily a bad thing in a major championship, it did prevent players from using their creativity and lessened the odds for fans to see great shots.

In 2013, Haigh is likely going to use a graduated rough, which will be more penal the farther a player misses the fairway, a philosophy that makes perfect sense. "The wider the shot, the more chance of being punished," he explained. "If you're just missing the fairways by a few feet, we want the players to be able to have a shot of some sort. Even though they may not be able to control the ball out of the rough to the green, we think it makes for more excitement, and it also allows the players with the skill who can manufacture the golf shot to be able to do so."

Corcoran likes the strategy, and he's not concerned at all that more players might finish under par. He said:

*It's all about philosophy and what type of tournament you want to provide. You can set up a golf course any way you want. We can go out there and set it up to where plus-five would be the winning score. People get the wrong impression from the standpoint of score and say if the winning score is minus-six, that Oak Hill isn't relevant anymore. That isn't the case at all. If we grow the rough right to the edges of the fairways and narrow those fairways, we can make the winning score be plus-five pretty easy.*

There are plenty of examples of this, such as Pebble Beach and Torrey Pines. Those venues host regular PGA Tour events every year in which the winning score is typically in the minus teens, sometimes even into the minus twenties. But when they host the U.S. Open, even-par is often a good score. "It's two totally different setups," said Corcoran. "Kerry doesn't have a misconception that he has to be at even-par for a championship. He doesn't care if the winning score is minus-four, minus-six or minus-eight. He's going to set it up to where it's going to be an entertaining championship."

And speaking of entertaining, there will be plenty of that going on in the fabulous Tudor-style clubhouse that, like the golf course, has undergone precipitous changes through the years to enable it to meet the needs of major championship hosting as well as day-to-day membership activity.

After the club hosted the Ryder Cup in 1995, the club made a tremendous investment—approximately $6 million—to perform a makeover of the clubhouse. Work began on the project in September 1996 and was completed in July 1997, as the square footage of the building was increased by eleven thousand feet to sixty-eight thousand. The result was a new formal dining room; a new grillroom, which was moved from the basement floor to the main level; a new ladies' locker room; a new 1,800-square-foot fitness center; and much-needed improvements to the guts of the structure, including new plumbing, air conditioning and heating.

Eric Rule, the club manager at the time, said the most impressive thing to him was that the character of the clubhouse really wasn't affected, as the building maintained its old-style architectural beauty while incorporating modern-day amenities in a seamless manner. "The only room that looks the same is the main ballroom, but as you walk from the new spaces to the old spaces, you don't notice the difference between the two," Rule remarked.

Embracing its century-plus of history, the board approved in 2008 the construction of a museum in the main hallway to the left of the front door, and it has become a must-see area for members and their guests. The display cases are filled with photos and artifacts that finely detail Oak

Dan Farrell took over as general manager of the club in 2012.

Hill's past. And across the hall, there is a room dedicated to the club's major championship history, as replicas of all the tournament trophies that have been awarded, including the Ryder Cup and the PGA Championship's Wanamaker Trophy, sit in beautifully adorned glass cases.

In 2013, a remodeling of the League of the Iroquois and Terrace rooms will add extra splendor and provide top-shelf space for corporate hospitality. "The clubhouse is being prepared not only for the PGA Championship being held this summer but also for future tournaments," said new club general manager Dan Farrell, who took over the operation in 2012. "Hosting future events is part of our DNA at the club, so we want to prepare in a positive and proactive way."

Farrell has worked in the golf industry for thirty years, but Oak Hill is the first club he has managed that has hosted a major championship. And though the workload is sometimes overwhelming, he's thrilled to be a part of it. "It's a different challenge, but it's truly an honor to be part of a national championship," he said. "Oak Hill is filled with tradition and golf history. It's a special place."

# Index

# About the Author

Sal Maiorana was born in Buffalo, New York, and grew up in the suburbs of Syracuse. He graduated from Buffalo State College in 1984 with a BA in journalism. After working part-time for the Associated Press, he landed his first job in the daily newspaper business at the *Leader* in Corning, New York. In 1986, he moved on to the *Rochester Democrat and Chronicle*, where he remains today. His primary responsibilities are covering the Buffalo Bills, golf and professional and college lacrosse and hockey.

Maiorana is the author of nineteen books, including the two-volume history of the Bills entitled *Relentless: The Hard-Hitting History of Buffalo Bills Football*, as well as two golf books: *Through The Green: The Art and Mind of a Professional Golfer*, with the cooperation of Davis Love III, and *Oak Hill Centennial: 1901–2001*. He was inducted into Rochester's Frontier Field Walk of Fame in 2009 and is a two-time winner of the Rochester Press-Radio Club Sportswriter of the Year award. He has also been recognized by the American Legion as Rochester's Sportswriter of the Year and has won numerous New York State Publishers' Association citations for his work with the *Democrat and Chronicle*.

Maiorana lives in Walworth with his wife, Christine; their two daughters, Taylor and Caroline; their son, Holden; and their dog, Buddy.